to Chr...

good Luck
Josef Perl
21/6/07

M000021387

Cover photograph, Calthorpe Park School, Hampshire, 29.6.2000

Faces in the Smoke

the story of Josef Perl
by
Arthur C Benjamin

First written and printed in 1998
by Arthur C Benjamin

Revised and edited by Frances Kahan and Sylvia Perl

Published in 2001 in Great Britain by Sylvia Perl,
1 Pinewood Lodge, Bushey Heath, Hertfordshire WD23 1EQ

ISBN 0-9541233-0-1

This book is the true story of part of Josef's life. It is written from
memory and some dates may be inexact.

Scanning and Reprographics by DX Imaging, Watford
Printed and bound by Martins the Printers Ltd,
Berwick-upon-Tweed.

To Ben Benjamin

and

Benjamin and Ella Kahan

"YOU ARE OUR FUTURE"

In memory of all the members of Josef's family
and all those who did not survive the
Holocaust

Acknowledgements

My sincere thanks to Arthur C Benjamin who wrote and printed the original 'Faces in the Smoke' and to his family who put up with his 'absence' for so many hours and days.

Heartfelt thanks to Frances, who worked tirelessly with me in revising, editing and typing her father's story.

Special thanks to her long-suffering husband, Albert, who uncomplainingly relinquished his hold on his computer and always managed to put things right when they went wrong.

Grateful thanks to our children Frances and Mark, without whose love and support over the years this book would not have been possible.

Sylvia Perl

"Behold the Tears of the Oppressed
and they had no-one to comfort them!

On the side of the Oppressors there was Power...
and I thought the dead more fortunate than the
living;

But better than both is he who has not yet been,
and has not seen the evil deeds that are done
under the sun."

Ecclesiastes 4:1-3

CONTENTS

PROLOGUE

The history of the Second World War learned from textbooks cannot convey the desperate struggle for survival during those times. Dates, treaties and statistics lie flat on the page. Numbers involved in the Holocaust are so enormous that they are beyond comprehension. The only way one can begin to understand them is to imagine, not six million men, women and children murdered, but to try and visualise one person, one family, one community, plus one, plus one, plus one...

When a Survivor tells you his story, history comes alive. You are with him on the edge of the pit looking down at the entangled bodies. You can see the enemy standing with his gun at the ready, signing the travel warrant, driving the train, erecting the fence. You see the prisoner helping others off a transport, doing any task that will enable him to live for another day, another hour, another minute. For what happened between 1938-45 was what one person did to another. Individualising gives a meaning that 'Six Million' cannot. You are forced to ask yourself "What would I have done? How would I have reacted and coped with such trauma?"

I have heard Josef Perl speak several times and had many conversations with him. Each time he has said something that makes me stop and think. After one of his talks a pupil asked, "How do you know what happened to the people?" His answer: "Because I saw their faces in the smoke."

Here, then, is the story of someone who lived a nightmare. The story of someone who, despite what the executioners thought, was destined to survive. The fact that you are reading the story at all is a tribute to what the human spirit can achieve. Josef once said to me, "I don't know why I was chosen by G-d to survive when so many others died."

The answer is before you now. It is to tell this story. May you learn as much from Josef as I have.

HOW THIS STORY CAME TO BE WRITTEN
or
ONE DAY IN JUNE

The release of the film 'Shindler's List' marked a turning-point in the teaching of the Holocaust. The film had made considerable impact on youngsters as Steven Spielberg had provided a video of it to all schools. For fifty years, the history of World War II had been taught in terms of military and political manoeuvres, but now the Government had put Holocaust studies firmly on our national educational curriculum.

Expanding on this recently-established aspect of study and linking RE with history, I decided in my school to organise 'Difference Day', a day on which I would concentrate on teaching the children the importance of racial harmony, of tolerance and the acceptance of one race for another. I would try to show how man's lust for power could play on people's unfounded and irrational fears and inadequacies until their apathy would lead to an acceptance of the bestial and inhuman horrors which were unfolding in every corner of their land.

A friend had mentioned that her father was a member of a synagogue in Bournemouth (my school is in Hampshire) and that several Holocaust Survivors were also members. What better way to educate than to have the children hear first-hand accounts of those who had suffered so much because of bigotry and mindless ignorance?

I telephoned the synagogue and in answer to my enquiry my name and number were passed on. A few days later, I received a call from Josef Perl's wife, Sylvia, who said her husband would be prepared to talk about his experiences and I explained about my plans for 'Difference Day'.

Sylvia passed the telephone to her husband, and for the first time I heard the voice with which I was to become so familiar. Standing in the hallway of my home, I heard how Josef and his father had met in Budapest 26 years after they had parted in a Polish forest. I only realised much later how much this telephone conversation was going to mean to me.

I was enormously pleased that he was willing to speak and had a great feeling of confidence, tempered with anxiety, as to how all my planning was going to come together on the 'Day'.

Not that there hadn't been a moment of panic. Some weeks before the agreed date I was leaving for school when the phone rang. It was Mrs Perl. She was sorry, but her husband had been unwell for some time and was now waiting to go into hospital for an operation. It now seemed likely that this would take place around the time that we were having our 'Difference Day' and she wanted me to have sufficient time to organise a replacement speaker. I *expressed my disappointment and my best wishes for a successful operation, but added that my invitation to the school still stood and if they were able to come as a visitor at the last moment they would be extremely welcome.*

PANIC! All the arrangements had been made. A whole year-group were involved, other speakers were booked, all of that day's lessons were cancelled so 150 pupils could take part in the 'Day'. Fortunately, I was able to find another speaker and the day went ahead as planned.

A few days before 'Difference Day', Mrs Perl phoned again. Joe had received the admission letter from the hospital. He was going in the day after 'Difference Day'.
"We know you have made other arrangements, but we would like to come just the same, Josef would like to meet you and the children."

Naturally, I readily agreed and so it was that on a sunny June morning a car, driven by a dark-haired lady, pulled into the school car park at about 10am, and a tall, grey-haired man, neatly dressed in grey trousers and a navy blazer opened the passenger door. As he climbed out I noticed that his left leg was rigid and, as they walked towards the school I realised this was not a recent injury.

I glanced around, reassuring myself yet again that everything was in place, before striding out to greet them. The five class-teachers had been working tirelessly to organise the day's programme and we were now nervously waiting for it all to start.

A lot was to change for me the day I walked down the school path. I held out my hand and introduced myself to "Mr Perl?"
"The name is Joe, and this is Sylvia. We are glad to be here."

The pupils had been split into four groups – drama, art, discussion group and listening to a Survivor's account. The timetable for the day enabled the pupils to experience each session. Two Survivors would speak twice, once in the morning and once after the lunch break. At the end of the day, all the pupils would assemble in the hall and, after a short play, a third Survivor would round up the day.

After the morning session, however, one of the speakers was not feeling strong enough to speak again, so Josef offered to take her place during the last session. And so I came to hear part of Joe's story for the first time.

DIFFERENCE DAY

The afternoon sessions were about to begin, and a group of excited pupils came thundering up the wooden stairs, shouting and shoving each other out of the way as they came flying through the narrow classroom door. Once inside, they rushed for the best seats - not the front row of course, no-one wants to be in the front row - as they all wanted to be in a spot where they could see and hear everything.

They had enjoyed the day so far. The drama session had been fun (partly because they hadn't had to wear uniform) and thought-provoking. The discussion had been more formal but had also allowed them to express their ideas more freely than in a normal class. The other session had been listening to a storyteller/poet read some of her work. Listening to the writer had given an extra lift to what on the page would just have been words. The day was certainly going well.

Now they were going to listen to a Survivor. They had begun their studies on the Second World War, heard about what had happened and read some historians' analyses. They had seen photographs of the camps, the lines of men on one side of the railway platform and the lines of women and children on the other. The smart uniforms of the Nazi guards had been in stark contrast to the bedraggled clothes of the people clutching their meagre possessions. The guards were all smiling confidently, clearly proud to let the world see what a fine job they were doing. The prisoners, on the other hand, looked bewildered and fearful. They had grown accustomed to taking orders, but up to this moment thought they had seen everything that could be devised to stamp them down, to make them feel they were worthless. These were people who, even though they did not know for certain, were hearing rumours and beginning to suspect that the unbelievable was about to happen. Had they been brought to this place to die?

The photographs of Jewish children particularly mystified the pupils. Somehow they appeared much older than they were. Their faces stared out from the grey scratched photographs and seemed to be looking at them, asking,
"Who are you on the other side of the camera? How is it that you are looking at us from a time that we were never allowed to see? You are in the future that should have belonged to us, and yet you look at us and see just an exercise in History or RE. Don't you realise that we are the parents of the friends that you were never to know, the adults who were never given the chance to know the world that you take so much for granted? Why do you just sit and look at the photographs and not see yourselves as you might have been, had you been born in Europe to Jewish parents?"

Over the lunch-hour, the pupils talked to their friends about what had happened so far in their different groups. There had been such a build-up to the day that they really were

20

expecting something unusual, and thankfully (from the teachers' point of view) it was turning out that way. Some had listened to a gentleman who had been forced to build V2 rockets. Others had heard the lady who had cried while telling her story, and had then said quietly,

"I won't tell you what the soldiers did to me when I was your age."

She didn't have to tell them, they understood that she had been raped many times. Yes, they had heard of it happening, but actually to be in the presence of someone who had been victim to it, a lady who looked like your own grandmother, subdued even the noisiest pupil. Whose story, the afternoon group wondered, would they hear?

There were a couple of teachers in the room, standing together to one side. They watched as the children settled themselves down. Some sat quietly waiting for the session to begin, others continued to make themselves heard by shouting at friends only a few seats away and one or two pulled out a book or a magazine and continued reading, lost in a world far away from school.

Unnoticed by the children, I entered the back of the room accompanied by the dark-haired lady and the grey-haired gentleman. The lady spoke quietly to her husband, gave his hand a squeeze, and then sat discreetly at the back. Josef and I headed towards the front of the class and as we did so the pupils, realising the talk was about to commence, fell silent.

"Thank you," I said. "I won't take up any of our speaker's time, and am pleased to introduce our guest, Mr Perl."

I walked to the side of the room, leaving Josef in charge of an audience of eager children. This is what they had come for, to listen to someone with a story to tell. Someone who could answer their questions and not just put them off with "I don't know" or "I'm not sure, but I'll try to find out." This man had first-hand experience, he had been one of those children on the other side of the camera lens but, unlike them, instead of just staring back he would tell them what happened.

Josef stood quietly for a moment, his hands clasped in front of him. His head was tipped slightly back and his eyes were closed as if in prayer - or was he looking back across the years for friends who could no longer speak for themselves, waiting for them to give him the nod, saying,
"Go on, Josef, tell them about us. Speak for those who no longer have a voice."
For a few seconds he remained still. The children held their breath, willing him to speak. He opened his eyes, looked around and began to recreate the world that he had watched being destroyed.

FOR THESE MEMORIES I AM GRATEFUL

My name is Josef Perl and I was born on 27th April 1930 in the town of Veliky Bochkov, which was then part of Czechoslovakia.

As a Survivor, I feel that I am a witness for both the living and the dead. Between 1938 and 1945 the greatest catastrophe in human existence befell the Jews of Europe, during which time six million Jewish people were killed in the most horrible ways. I cannot come to terms with the fact that, while all of the carnage was going on, the free people of the world stood by and said nothing.

Out of those six million Jews, one-and-a-half million were children. They had no chance to live, to laugh, to learn to read and write, to study to become scientists, doctors, professors who could contribute so brilliantly, as we Jews have done throughout our history. They did not have the opportunity to grow up and find themselves in the position that I am in now - telling you the story of what happened to me and how I came to be here.

I want to tell you a little bit about myself, about my background. Before I do, I would like you to please remember I was only eight years old when all this started happening, much younger than you are now. I come from an orthodox family, not fanatically religious, but we took our religion seriously. My parents, Frieda and Lazar, had nine children. I was the eighth child, and the only son. My father ran a sawmill and dealt in wood and we lived in a smallholding with many animals. Like all the Jewish children, I went to Cheder[1] twice a day. I remember very well how every Friday morning Rabbis would come to our Cheder from other areas and test us to see what we had learned throughout the week. Goodness only knows what would have happened if I had got a 'C', but because I enjoyed my religious instruction so greatly, I always did well, and my father was pleased with me. Education was an important part of my life, as it is in any Jewish family. Each day, I would go to Cheder from 6am until 7.30am and then go to state school from 8am until 4pm. It was back to Cheder from 4.30 until 7pm, followed by synagogue service until 7.30pm. I would return home for the evening meal, after which there was always some homework to be done. As you can see, there was not a lot of free time, but I remember my early childhood as being happy. I was part of a warm, loving family and for these memories I am grateful.

One evening when we were reciting prayers together, my father noticed that I was not looking at the book.
"Are you reading those prayers," he asked me, "or are you just saying them because you remember them?"
"Of course I am reading them," I replied unconvincingly.
"Then show me exactly where we are on the page," he challenged.

---

[1] classes for religious studies

My father was right, of course. I had learned it all by heart and so I struggled vainly to find the correct place in the prayer book. My father went to the Rabbi and said that he didn't want me to learn 'parrot fashion', but that I should always read properly and know what I was reading. Furthermore, the Rabbi was to discipline me if necessary.

The Rabbi seemed to take him at his word, for the next time I did not satisfy him he brought out his stick which was about as thick as your thumb and gave me an almighty whack across the shoulders with it! At home that night, when I was washing before bed, my mother noticed this great big bruise across my back and asked me how I had got it. Not daring to tell her the truth, I said that I had fallen over.
"Don't give me that nonsense," she said, "that isn't the kind of bruise you get from falling. What has happened?"
When she persisted, I told her that one of my friends had done it to me. At this, she became very angry and threatened to do terrible things to my friend. Clearly, I couldn't let him take the blame and so I told her about the Rabbi. This made her even angrier. No-one was going to do that to her boy, and so she took me to him and left him in no doubt as to what would happen to him if he so much as laid a finger on me. Poor Rabbi! He was a very small man and my mother was a very large lady with a formidable character. He never hit me again, but he taught me well.

I always had a good relationship with my father. He was a hardworking, intelligent man and he never told me what to do without explaining everything to me. I was his only son, and he treated me as an equal and for this I admired and respected him. I especially remember how he would often explain things to us by telling us a parable, a story, so that we could understand. To me, he was someone to look up to, but he was more than that. He always tried to lift me up to his level so that I could become like him and carry on the family name. When he went to a meeting, he would often take me along. If businessmen came to our home for maths lessons with my father, he always sat me next to him so that I too would learn. He treated me as an adult.

Other people in our community also respected my father. Often when there was a dispute, the people concerned would seek out my father and ask him to mediate. So great was their respect for him, that they would invariably accept his decision.

While I was growing up, there were always discussions about our future, especially about my sisters'. My eldest sister had married before I was born and, when I was about three years old, two of my sisters married on the same day. My mother was one of five children – she had two brothers and two sisters. My father was one of eight and had four brothers and three sisters. They all came to celebrate the double wedding with their children and grandchildren. Together with all our neighbours and friends, you can imagine what a joyous wedding that was.

Another sister, Sara, left home to study nursing in a Budapest hospital. This was something my father had to come to terms with as it meant she would have to work on the Sabbath. I don't think he was very happy about it, but she had made up her mind - Sara wanted to be a nurse, and so she left. I thought of her often and constantly played at being a doctor, taking temperatures, bandaging people's arms and so on. I told my father I, too, would like to study medicine when I grew up. It was not to be, of course, but I often ask myself what our family would have achieved had the war not intervened.

We lived in a large house adjacent to the synagogue and owned our own Sefer Torah[1] that had been handed down through the generations from my great-grandfather. On Simchat Torah[2], one of the most joyous festivals in the Jewish calendar, the Torah would be brought home from the synagogue and our family and friends would come in to read it together. There would be great rejoicing and we would dance and sing and have a meal. We were a happy family and shared our happiness with others. I knew only goodness from my parents and what good I do now I first learned from them.

When I was unwell, my mother would feed me hourly with tiny portions of bread and butter. On one occasion when I was extremely ill, the Rabbi was sent for to give me a blessing. He brought with him a little bag containing religious objects to wear around my neck, hoping that their mystic powers would speed my recovery. I remember waking up and seeing my father seated beside me.
"Josef," he asked, "what can I get you?"

---

[1] A holy parchment scroll containing the first five books of the Old Testament (The Pentateuch).
[2] An annual festival which celebrates having read through the Torah to the final portion.

"Grapes, please," I replied.

Now, in those days, grapes were not easily obtainable, but the next time I awoke, there they were!

Another of my childhood memories was one time when my mother had been baking. One of my sisters and I were fighting over who was to taste the cake first. We argued for so long that my mother was beside herself. She pushed us away, but I fell and caught the side of my face on a chair. Indeed, a tooth, which had been giving me a great deal of pain for several days, had been knocked out. The pain had gone. Even when she was angry with me, my mother still carried out a kind deed!

Every Friday morning my mother would prepare our family's food for the Sabbath, but she would make more than we could ever eat. This was because she always made enough for visitors and also for the poorer people she knew would be calling. In fact, people came to our home because they knew there would always be a welcoming meal for them. My father was respected for his wisdom and my mother for her goodness to others.

I clearly remember collecting fruit from our orchard - apples, pears, cherries, whatever was available. We would put them into a huge pot, which was left to simmer overnight. Next day, the mixture would be poured out onto shallow trays and left to cool. Soon, it hardened and looked like leather, and would be cut into strips and wrapped. This was how my mother preserved the fruit for the winter, though much of it was given away. To make a wonderful, fruity jam, all one had to do was boil it up again with a little water. Delicious!

My eldest sister Frimid, and her husband, Mordechai, had considerable difficulties having a child. Frimid had many miscarriages, and this was a great sorrow to them. Eventually she succeeded in carrying a child to term and you can imagine their joy, the joy of the whole family, when their son, Ezra, was born.

Unfortunately, soon after his birth in 1937, it became increasingly clear that all was not well: he kept losing consciousness. My father told me,
"Joe, before and after school each day, please go to Frimid's house and pray for Ezra."
As my father's work took him away from home, sometimes for days at a time, and being a dutiful son, I naturally did as he asked me. I would sit by the baby's cradle for hours, pulling its string to rock him to sleep whilst I recited Psalms. Every so often, I would gently put my hand onto his head so that he would know I was there with him, looking after him. After six or seven months of this, Ezra seemed much stronger and so, one day, instead of going to see him, I went straight to Cheder. Afterwards, as evening prayers were beginning, someone came rushing in.
"Joe, Joe, you must come at once! Little Ezra has fainted again. He still needs your prayers."

I left the synagogue immediately and rushed to my nephew's side. For another year I visited him daily and offered my prayers while I comforted him. This continued until he was almost two years old, when he seemed to have recovered fully. During this time, and although I was only young myself, I developed a very close relationship with him. As he grew older, it became obvious that he was developing into a highly intelligent child, wise beyond his years and when he was only three he could read Hebrew well enough to ask his grandfather the 'Ma Nishtanah'[1] at the Passover[2] Seder[3].

As I have already told you, I had a very happy childhood. In my part of the world there was very little anti-Semitism. At school, where about one quarter of the children were Jewish, we all played happily and harmoniously together, Jews and Christians. Three of my cousins, who were also called Josef, went to the same school and we were known as 'The Four Joes'. If any of our friends were in trouble they would tell the troublemaker, "I'll tell the Joes!" and that was usually enough to stop anything. Once, when a boy was bullying one of my friends, I decided to teach him a lesson. I persuaded a friend to encourage the boy to steal fruit from our orchard and I loosened two struts from the fence so he would be able to get in quite easily. He fell into the trap and entered the orchard, where he proceeded to scoop up as much fruit as he could carry, greedily filling his clothes to bursting. When he tried to leave, laden down with his spoils he became stuck in the fence! That was my chance, and I gave him a good hiding. He couldn't really complain to anyone, as he would have had to admit he had been stealing. We had no more trouble with him after that. (I remembered this

---

[1] During the Passover Seder, the youngest child present traditionally asks 'Four Questions' of the head of the family about the festival. The first two words of this in Hebrew are 'Ma Nishtanah'.
[2] Passover commemorates the Jewish people's freedom from slavery under Pharaoh's Egypt. The festival lasts eight days.
[3] The ceremonial meal, and story of Passover, which takes place on the first two nights of the festival.

lesson about not trying to carry too much, as you will hear later.)

Winters in that part of the world were really, really cold and harsh. Some days, it was so cold that when I arrived at school there were icicles hanging from my eyelashes. Sometimes, my mother would give me two freshly baked potatoes for my lunch and I would hold them in my hands, which were stuffed deep into my pockets, to keep them warm.

My mother used to bake bread every day. Sometimes, when I didn't have time between school and cheder to go home, I would go to a local shop where I could get a snack and put it on my father's account. I would often choose bread and a bar of chocolate. Years later, when I emerged from the camps, one of my greatest delights was not having to fight for every crumb. Yes, bread is very important.

We had a variety of animals – goats, sheep, chickens, cows, and horses. I was about five-and-a-half years old when my father called me into the stable to watch a foal being born. He asked me if I would like to have a horse of my own. Of course, I said yes, and he said the foal would be mine as soon as it was old enough to leave its mother. This foal, Shari, and an Alsatian dog called Bondi were my best friends. I understood them and they understood me. Even though we did not talk in a way that other people would comprehend, we each knew what the other was thinking and we went everywhere together. I rode Shari without a saddle and can still feel her backbone because, after a ride of several miles to school,

I used to be sore where I bounced every time she took a step. Every day I would ride to school on Shari, Bondi running along beside us, and then they would go home. Later in the day, they would both come back to collect me so that I could ride home again. One day when we were away from home, I fell and hurt myself. I was in such pain that I couldn't manage to climb onto her back. Do you know what she did? She lay down on her side so that I could get my leg across her. She got onto her knees and then stood upright with me hanging onto her mane. Then we all went home.

They were carefree days but they were not to last.

THE SPRING OF 1940

In 1933, Hitler had become Chancellor of Germany. His National Socialist party, or Nazi party, wanted to restore Germany to what they perceived as their 'rightful' place in Europe. They sought world domination. Austria was annexed in the 'Anschluss' of March 1938. Fearing for its sovereignty, Czechoslovakia mobilised its military in May of that year, but had no support from its European allies. In fact, in September 1938 at the Munich Conference, Britain (Neville Chamberlain), France (Daladier) and Italy (Benito Mussolini) granted Czechoslovakia's Sudetenland to Hitler, in their policy to appease Hitler and so avoid war.

Meanwhile, in Germany itself, on 9 November 1938 the Nazi authorities orchestrated a nationwide pogrom against the Jewish population, destroying shops, homes and over 200 synagogues. Twenty thousand Jews were arrested in what became known as 'Kristallnacht', the Night of Broken Glass. From that time on, Jews were forbidden to hold driving licences, visit theatres, concert halls, cinemas, they could sit only on designated benches in parks, shop only during certain hours of the day and a nightly curfew was imposed.

Also in 1938, Hungary and Germany signed a peace treaty. Admiral Horthy, the Hungarian Head of State, who admired Hitler, supporting and passing his anti-Jewish laws, thought this treaty had given Hungary equal status with Germany. Rumours were abounding about deportations and unspeakable suffering in far-off places. It was also said that if one could prove Hungarian citizenship one would be safe, so my father, who had been an officer in the Hungarian Army during the First World War, went to Budapest to have his Hungarian papers validated. This rumour turned out to be totally unfounded.

I had started school when I was five years old. Three years later, in 1938, a short while after the peace treaty had been signed, our teachers were dismissed and replaced by Hungarian teachers who had been specifically trained in Nazi ideology. When we arrived at school, instead of sitting in our usual places with our friends, we were told where to sit. We were all, Jews and Christians alike, confused and bewildered. Suddenly we were told we were different, and that we were to be segregated. Jews sat on one side of the classroom and Christians sat on the other. It soon became evident that these new teachers were indoctrinating the non-Jewish children to hate us. Our calm, happy, peaceful world was shattered.

Within two or three days, children who had been my friends and with whom I had played all my school days would no longer talk to me. When I approached one of them, he spat,
"Don't come near me, you dirty Jew!"

Older children began to harass Jewish children and to make our lives miserable, waiting for us outside school and beating us up as we left. We tried everything to avoid trouble and I remember many occasions when we 'Four Joes' jumped out of an upstairs window onto the snow just before the end of lessons so we could be out of the building before the bigger pupils caught us. I told my parents what was happening, but my father insisted I try and carry on going to school and continuing my education as long as possible.

The laws restricting Jewish freedom of movement in Germany were now being enforced in Czechoslovakia. During this time, soldiers had been looking around the homes of Jewish people, sizing them up. On one visit to our house, they told me I had no need for a dog, and promptly shot Bondi. They left, taking my beloved Shari with them. I was heartbroken.

From then on, I had to walk to school. There was no public transport and school was about five miles away. After almost a year of putting up with the bullying at school, I was walking home one day when I saw scores of Hungarian soldiers sitting at the side of the road. They immediately knew I was Jewish because I had the traditional 'peyers'[1] and wore a skullcap. One of them, encouraged by his friends, came over to me. Pulling out his bayonet he cut off my curls. They all found this highly amusing. I was mortified and humiliated. I felt as if I had lost an arm, as my 'peyers' were very much a part of me and I couldn't understand why anyone would want to do

---

[1] Sidelocks worn by orthodox Jewish males.

this. Why should a group of armed men amuse themselves by picking on a child?

I cried the rest of the way and, when I arrived home, told my parents that I would not go back to school any more. After that, I only attended Cheder, which was being run clandestinely. My formal education ended when I was eight-and-a-half years old.

Sometimes when we were sitting round the table at home, our thoughts and conversations turned to the uncertainty of what lay ahead for us. We would talk to our friends and neighbours about what we should do in the future. It was decided that our most precious possession, our Sefer Torah, should be hidden in a safe place. There were other families in the community who also had their own Sefer Torahs and it was decided that we would wrap them as best we could and bury them in our gardens. Hopefully, they would remain safely hidden until the end of those anxious times. Life struggled on, with ever-increasing restrictions being imposed on the Jewish population.

Our troubled lives were echoes of the grander political events taking place in Western Europe. On 1st September, 1939, despite Hitler's promises to the European alliance, Germany invaded Poland. Britain, who had given assurances of protection to Poland, had no option but to declare war on Germany, which Chamberlain did on 3rd September. Europe was at war.

One day in the spring of 1940, at Passover-time, an uneasy, quiet tension descended on our town. It was the calm before the storm. Something was going to happen. We had no idea what that something might be, and no-one in civilised humanity would ever, in their wildest imagination, have pictured what was to come.

We lived in the heart of our town, on the main road. On that dreadful day, Hungarian militia, working under the command of the Germans, suddenly surrounded all the Jewish homes in the centre of town. This, we discovered later, was designed to enable them to control the area without alerting too many local people before they had established their power base. Everyone was told to report to the synagogue in three hours' time, where a census would be carried out. We were told we wouldn't be away from our homes for very long, but could take food and blankets with us.
"No need to lock your doors," we were told. "You will only be away from home a short while."

Five long years later, when I returned to my home, I realised exactly why we had to leave our doors open and our valuables behind. Our homes had been ransacked and non-Jewish people had taken them for their own. Even after the war, some of those who managed to survive and returned to their hometowns were unable to reclaim their homes and many were even killed by the inhabitants who did not want to give up their newly-acquired houses.

Although we had been told not to be afraid, we left our homes apprehensively, and nervously made our way into the synagogue. The old, the sick, toddlers, even the new-born, no-one was exempt. When we reached the synagogue it was full to bursting and many people had to stay outside.   Even the building that housed the 'Mikveh'[1] was packed with people. Soon the children began to cry. They were growing tired and could feel the tension mounting. Meanwhile, there was no sign of anyone taking a census. In fact, no list was ever made of our group. As it turned out, this was unusual for the Germans, who were normally so meticulous at record-keeping.

Suddenly, at 4am, there was a great commotion.   The doors crashed open and Hungarian soldiers with an officer of the German SS in charge came rushing into the synagogue with dogs and carrying batons and guns. All hell let loose.   There was shouting and screaming as everyone was ordered out.

"Raus! Raus!" (Out! Out!)
"Schnell! Schnell!" (Quick! Quick!)

Everyone was pushed and shoved, kicked and beaten in the direction of the railway station. Some people tried to snatch up their blankets but dropped them on the way. Others stumbled over them.   In the frenzied confusion, mothers lost hold of their children. If they were lucky, they managed to find them again, but sometimes the pressure of the people behind would push them over as they bent down, causing a great pile of struggling people trying to get to their feet, accompanied by kicks and blows from clubs and rifle butts beating down on them. All of this was accompanied by the shrieks of parents calling out for the children who were lost and the terrified cries of children calling for their parents. Stumbling along as best they could were the old and infirm who, often, were the first to

---

[1] Ritual baths adjacent to the synagogue.

go under. At the station a train of cattle wagons was waiting for us. These wagons were several feet off the ground and, as there were no steps or ramps to help you, you had to climb in as best you could. Everyone wanted to get in, hoping to escape the violence they had been enduring since leaving the synagogue. But clambering into the wagons was far from easy. The first men who jumped in helped to pull up those behind them. Women's dresses were torn, men's trousers ripped, and their legs injured where they caught themselves on splintered wood and torn metal. Soon the sides of the wagons were streaked with blood.

Once in, I peered out through a gap in the planks, trying vainly to comprehend the horrors I was witnessing. The children, who had been lost along the way and were crying and searching for their mothers, arrived at the station last. Incensed at the sight of them, I saw one soldier grab a toddler by one arm and, swinging him around his head, tossed him into the nearest wagon. Who knows if he was ever reunited with his mother? In the road, I could see a few belongings abandoned, as were the dead and dying.

After what seemed like an eternity, silence descended. Even the children and babies stopped crying as we waited in fear to see what was going to happen next.

MOSHIACH[1] WILL HELP US

Josef stopped speaking.   His eyes were closed and, although he was physically in the room with us, in his mind he was once more that ten year-old child, peering through a gap in the cattle wagon's side.   He was looking out at a once-familiar place, but the scene he was now witnessing was horrifying and would stay with him forever.   The old happy world of football and games with his friends had evaporated and been brutally replaced by scenes of dead and injured lying on the street of his hometown.   The houses and trees were no longer the background of a secure world; the friends he had known for most of his life were gone.

Some townspeople who, by their passiveness, gave tacit consent to the violence inflicted on their neighbours, had become part of the horror by standing by while others carried out their hideous task.   When deeds of this nature occur, there are no 'innocent' bystanders; we are all participants to some degree.

I looked around at the pupils.   Even the most vocal were silent, those who could usually be relied upon to make

---

[1] The Hebrew word for the 'Messiah'.

some comment or another, for once had nothing to say. It was one of those moments when even the most insensitive was moved and absorbed by the story unfolding. They were all staring, transfixed, some with looks of horror on their faces, other with tears in their eyes as they imagined that they were this boy, peering out onto the platform.

Josef opened his eyes, looked at his audience, and proceeded to take them with him on his journey.

Packed into the wagons like sardines, with no room to move, we looked at each other in silence. What could anyone say? There was no water and no sanitation. The doors were closed and locked. The only air was through a small opening in the side of the wagon, stuffed with barbed wire. Eventually, the train started to move slowly forward with a clunk, a jerk and a hissing out of steam. We were all afraid to speak, but after a while the tension relaxed a little and some began to cry. Four of my sisters had not been at home when we were taken away. Two were working in Budapest and the other two were on a visit to them. Now, in the wagon, I was with my mother, father, my younger sister Priva, and my three oldest sisters, Frimid, Rivka and Leah, and their five children. I felt comforted by this, as most other families had been separated.

How quickly we children grew up that day. Ezra, who was now three years old, was in his mother's arms. He took her tear-stained face between his hands and said, "Don't cry Mummy, Moshiach will help us." In that moment, I realised how the world had been turned upside down. Whilst it should have been the parents comforting the children, children were now comforting their parents.

We were crammed onto that train, tightly packed together. You can't imagine what it was like - unable to move we had to perform all of our bodily functions where we were. Some people fainted, a few suffered heart attacks, others died, but they had to remain in the wagon with us for the next two days and nights. The air was foul.

Eventually the train stopped, deep inside a forest, somewhere in Poland. The wagon doors were unlocked and we were forced off the train with kicks and blows. The guards were bellowing at us to move quickly. We found ourselves in a clearing in which had been erected a huge circus-like tent, surrounded by barbed wire, but not electric wire. The first people to go inside the tent were so exhausted that, rather than go right to the other side, they simply collapsed by the entrance. As more and more of us were pushed in, those who were coming in behind had to try and climb over them in order to find a place for themselves. People tripped and fell on those who were already on the ground and scores of people were crushed to death. It was always to be that way: any movement ordered had to take place at double speed, and the weakest always died.

In any group of people there are those who naturally come forward to try and help others and themselves. As was to become the norm, we were without food, water or sanitation. Some of the men formed a delegation and asked the guard if they could speak to the Commandant. They wanted to ask for shovels so they could organise some form of sanitation at least. The guard went to the Commandant's tent, which had been erected outside the perimeter wire. The Commandant appeared and beckoned them to him, as if he intended to speak to them. They stopped as they reached the wire, but he once more beckoned them through. Instead of speaking to them, he ordered the men to line up. Then, turning to the guards he barked,

"Shoot them all!"

We had all been watching and were stunned by this brutal act. Although by now I had seen many dead and dying, I had never seen anyone shot before. It brought back to me a saying my father often repeated - "a man is as strong as iron, but as weak as a fly." In that moment, I had seen healthy men brought down by the violence of a tiny bullet. I learned a lot about our captors that day.

Bodies lay where they fell for two days, while our captors organised themselves. They partitioned off a small area inside the tent for the purpose of searching us. We were made to undress and, fifty at a time, we had to pick up our bundles of clothing and go in front of the German Commandant and the guards. The guards were actually Polish, but wearing German uniforms. We spread our bundles on a table and the guards, supervised by SS officers, searched us. Anything that was found to be of value was handed to the SS. They were convinced that all Jews were wealthy and carried gold and jewels hidden about their person and so their methods of conducting a search were always brutal and cruel. I had some paper money hidden in the peak of my cap and when I saw how the others were being searched I pretended to throw a childish tantrum. When my turn came, I ripped my cap off of my head and threw it to the ground kicking and screaming. While a guard was struggling with me, I kicked the cap so it flew away from us and was ignored. By the time the search was over I was, much to the guards amusement, in tears and, as soon as I was released, I scuttled around picking up my clothes, which were all over the place. In the chaos they did not realise that they had missed the cap and so I ran off with the money that was to prove very useful later, as we soon found out that some of the guards were not above a little bribery.

Having been without any nourishment since entering the wagon, the pains of hunger were becoming unbearable. The little food we had managed to bring with us when we left home had long since been eaten. After a couple of days, I went to my father and said I was going to sneak out under the wire and see if I could find some food.
"The forest can't last for ever," I said to him. "When I get to some fields I am bound to find something for us to eat. I'll be back before daybreak."

Word soon spread that I was planning my search, and soon seven other boys joined me and whispered,
"If you're going, we're coming too!"
"Okay," I said, "but we can't all go together. We'll go out two at a time, at five-minute intervals. And remember – if anyone gets caught, you did this on your own!"

It took us a while to reach the edge of the forest, where we found cultivated fields, just as I had expected. There were all sorts of vegetables growing. We tied the bottoms of our trouser legs so that we could carry as much as possible.

Remembering the day I had tempted a boy into our orchard, I warned them not to overload themselves.

"Don't forget," I warned, "you still have to crawl back under that wire!"

When we returned, we were pleased with our bounty. Each boy went back to his family and we shared the food with those near to us. As if by magic, pots appeared. There was, of course, plenty of firewood around as we were surrounded by trees, and our pipe-smokers still had their matches on them. Someone must have collected water from a nearby stream, and before we knew it, my mother had a pot of soup boiling. Every fourth night, for about six weeks, we repeated our sortie. We ate for two days, starved for two days, and then went out again.

One day during our first week in the tent, my father and I were witness to an event that was to have a profound effect on us. For some reason, a boy of about my own age had got into trouble. One of the Polish guards was beating him to a pulp. When his father tried to protect him they had both been summarily killed. I clutched my father in horror. We went into a corner and talked about it. Reluctantly we agreed that, if one of us fell into trouble – and I was sure I would – the other would not come and help. This way, one of us might survive.

One evening, when I was preparing to sneak out again, my father called me to him.

"Yossel[1]," he said, "before you go out tonight, I want to do something that under normal conditions would not happen

---

[1] Affectionate Yiddish term for Josef.

until you became Bar Mitzvah[1]. I want to bestow upon you the blessing the Rabbi would give you when you become a man. You are already carrying out the duties and responsibilities of a man, and G-d only knows when we will see each other again."

So saying, he put his hands on my head and blessed me. What did he mean, "when we will see each other again" I wondered? I was going under the wire and would be back before morning. But my mind was too busy with plans for my evening escapade to ponder this further.

That night, we were picking our way back in the dark and just approaching the camp when we heard a great commotion. It was too dark to see much at first, but the terrible noises of screaming, crying, gun shots and barking dogs carried clearly in the night air and stopped us in our tracks. We hid behind some trees, near enough to watch, aghast, as everyone was being forced into the lorries and driven away. It was a long time before all the people had been removed from the tent and the last of the guards and lorries had departed.

When everything had gone quiet we crept out of hiding and went down to the camp. Those who had been too old, or too young, or too weak to jump on the lorries were strewn on the ground like so much rubbish that was of no further use to our captors. They had shot those left behind mercilessly, but some were not quite dead. Carefully, with tears running down our cheeks, we turned the bodies over, searching vainly for our loved ones among these poor people.

---

[1] Confirmation of a boy when he reaches manhood, at the age of 13.

Feeling helpless, we went back into the forest and, having a great need to stay together, remained there for a week, until all our food had gone. We talked constantly about our families, wondering what had happened to them. Certain in the knowledge that eight Jewish boys together would soon be spotted and caught, we decided to set off individually and look for our families. What happened to the others I have no idea, I never saw any of them again.

For the next year, I wandered around Poland, picking up a trail here, another one there, following one rumour after another, always hoping to find my family. It was a hard, dangerous life, living rough, eating any food I could obtain. I had been anxious to find a gang of boys so I could conceal myself amongst them and not stand out. I had soon come across a gang of Polish boys. When they asked me who I was, I said I was Czech, and they had accepted me warily. I needed to keep my wits about me to make sure I didn't give myself away as any word, any sign that I understood Yiddish[1] might betray me, because these boys spoke it fluently. Sometimes, when they were planning a raid, they would talk in Yiddish, thinking I couldn't understand. They would loot Jewish houses and steal food. These boys had a fierce hatred of Jews, and I can easily think of them as people who, once the war was over, would kill any survivors who returned home. There are many examples of Poles 'finishing Hitler's work for him'.

By constantly keeping my wits about me, and being on the move, I was sure I would eventually be reunited with my family. I would go into a town and ask questions, follow

---

[1] Language used by Jews in Central and Eastern Europe.

leads: there would always be a snippet of information that was worth following up. Being able to speak Czech, Hungarian, Polish, Russian, German and of course Yiddish, I could easily blend in wherever I went.

Soon it became clear that it was getting too dangerous for me to stay with the gang I was with - they were growing more vicious and, at the same time, more suspicious of me. Then, one day, I came across a German army camp. Near the gates were some horses. Intending to free myself from the gang, I wandered into the camp towards the horses and started patting one of them. A German soldier was nearby.

"What a beautiful horse he is," I said.

"Do you like horses?" the soldier asked.

"Oh, yes. If you give me a brush I'll groom him for you."

When I had finished grooming two horses, the soldier came over and invited me to sit down and eat the soup he had brought for me. Imagine - hot soup! It was the first hot food I had eaten for months. As I started to eat, two of the soldiers standing nearby were talking about their day's work.

"I'm so tired, we've had a very busy day," said one soldier. "We took scores of Jews from that ghetto over there and killed them," he said, waving his arm to the left. The other soldier shrugged.

"Why are you so tired? We took hundreds of Jews from that ghetto and killed them," he was pointing in a different direction.

I had just taken my first spoon of soup and started choking on it. These very men I was sitting near were the men that were killing my people - maybe my family had been slaughtered by them today. I felt the colour drain from my face. I had to get away. I put down my spoon, excused myself and hurried out of their camp.

The soldiers had indicated the direction of the ghettos, and I set off towards one of them. Ghettos were areas within a town into which all the Jews were forced to live, separated from the rest of the town and sealed off, the perimeters being guarded by armed German soldiers. There was no regular food or other provisions sent in – no water, medicines etc. The Jews were not allowed out of the ghetto, but the youngsters had their ways of escaping under fences and in sewers to scavenge for food and supplies for their families. Conditions were extremely poor and the weakest did not survive for long.

The Germans would offer food or favours to some of the men if they volunteered to help organise the ghetto. In this way, they organised a so-called Jewish 'police force' within the ghetto. Then the Germans would say derisively, "Look how these Jews behave when left to organise themselves – they aren't fit to live!"
A Jewish policeman was distinguishable by the blue band around his hat.

Eventually, I found myself outside a ghetto. I do not know where I was as I had by now spent almost a year wandering around Poland, but I do remember it being late summer of 1941. There was a Jewish policeman on duty at the gates and the small band of Polish boys I had attached myself to at that time started throwing stones at him and calling him names. I joined in, discreetly moving closer to him. When he started to chase us away, I made sure I was caught and, while he was shaking me, I spoke to him quickly in Yiddish.

"Don't stop hitting me, but listen! I'm Jewish and I'm trying to get into the ghetto to find my family."

"I don't want to know the details," he hissed hurriedly. "There's an SS guard on duty over there watching me, and I have to take you in. When we get to the gate I'll throw you inside. Once in, roll over, get up and run as fast as you can. Don't let that guard have a chance to pull out his gun and shoot you!"

He had me by the scruff of my neck and, as he threw me in, he was shouting to the SS and complaining about the behaviour of the Polish children. I went flying into the ghetto and ran off as fast as my legs would take me.

I stopped, unable to run any more. I was tired and breathless, but realised it was the stench that was choking me. Looking around, I was sickened to see the squalid conditions and the dilapidated state of the places where the people lived. Windows were broken, doors had obviously been used for firewood to make a little warmth, buildings were falling apart, and I couldn't believe that anyone was actually living here. Then I saw the people. Those walking around looked like zombies, all skin and bone, their eyes dull and lifeless. They looked almost dead, but were still clinging to life. Many were lying around on the pavements, on the ground, already dead. I thought I had landed in Hell.

I saw one man who was so weak he could only move by leaning up against the wall. Sitting on a doorstep not far away from me was a woman trying to feed a baby. As I stood there, her arms fell to her sides and the baby dropped to the ground where it lay whimpering. The mother had died and there was no-one there to help the baby. What kind of a place was this? How could people be dehumanised in this way? How could they be left to die in these conditions?

I stood there, not knowing what to do next. Could my family possibly be amongst these people? I looked around and saw an old man inside a house beckoning me towards him. As I neared him, he pulled me inside by the arm.
"Who are you?" he asked. "You don't belong here. Get out! Get out, while you can! Don't you realise that every day in here hundreds of people are dying."
Without calling anyone, another man suddenly appeared at my side.
"Come on," he said, "I'm going to get you out of here."

He led me through the sewers, wading ankle and sometimes waist-deep through the muck and filth, with rats swimming alongside of us, until we were under the wall and beyond the perimeter of the ghetto, where he left me. I soon came across a stream where I was able to wash my clothes and myself. Donning these still wet clothes I made my way out into the countryside again to continue my search.

After about six weeks of wandering about, surviving I don't know how, I neared a prison camp. I was wondering how to get in and look around, when suddenly I heard a click behind me. I didn't turn round as I knew there was a gun to my head. Instinctively, I put my hands in the air and the SS officer marched me towards the camp. We had gone only a short way when I saw a column of naked men, women and children, being marched out, hundreds of them, five abreast.

"Stop! Strip!" the guard ordered.

I had no alternative and, when I was naked, he pushed me in amongst them and we were marching, in bitter cold, deep into the forest. We were stopped alongside a huge, long pit, which had been dug out. It was giving off a cloud of white vapour. What was causing this I don't know. The whole scene was unreal. At first, I heard the rat-a-tat of machine gunfire. We knew what must be happening, but in another way, could not believe that we were all going to die today and be lying in that pit. The shots gradually became louder as the column shortened. After a while, I could see the people fall into the pit. Then, as I neared the front of the column, I could clearly see what was happening to each row of five. They were brought forward to stand on the edge of the trench. With their backs towards the soldiers, they were shot and fell into the pit, and the next group was brought forward. While guards were aligning them, the soldiers with machine guns casually sipped hot drinks for warmth. To them it was just another day's work.

As I neared the pit, I began to distinguish the features of those who were dying in front of me and whom I expected to be joining soon. Then, when I was about seven rows from the front, to my horror I recognised the whole row. It was my mother. My mother and four of my sisters. I wanted to call out, to let them know I was there, to say goodbye – rat-a-tat – it was too late: they were gone.

I was fixed to the spot. My eyes, my hands, my feet, nothing would move. Then the next row of five moved forward. My little niece and nephews, the children I had played with, including Ezra, who had fought so hard for life and who had shown his mother how to hope, were all ushered to the edge of the pit.

"Hold hands! Hold hands!" ordered their murderers.

And with that they shot them in the back. The bullets hit them with such force that the little ones were thrown three feet into the air before falling into the trench.

At that moment I felt the world had unhinged itself.

A LITTLE BOY RUNNING

I looked around the room. Like me, the pupils were sitting in stunned silence. I had read many books on the subject of the Holocaust and had come across many harrowing descriptions of life in the ghettos and camps, so I was not expecting that the story this Survivor would tell would affect me so strongly. Reading accounts of the atrocious events could, however, in no way compare to listening to a man who had endured the unimaginable and yet remained an upstanding, understanding and tolerant human being.

Josef had lived through experiences as a child that no-one should ever have to bear. I had tried to inform my pupils about the Shoah[1], presenting them with the facts and trying not to be too emotional about a very emotive subject. Now, as I looked round the hall at my pupils, I could sense the tension mounting as the children identified with that young lad in the forest.

Josef began to speak again.

Soon it would be my turn to step forward and die. Suddenly an air-raid siren sounded and the order was given for us all to lie face-down on the ground. Instead,

---

[1] Hebrew word for The Holocaust.

everyone began to run higgledy-piggledy all over the place. What was there to lose now? I ran straight into the forest.

I ran and ran. Eventually I heard voices of men talking as they worked. I stopped, my mind in turmoil. I could hardly take in the events of the last few hours. Now here I was, naked and alone, knowing that I would never see half of my family again. But time was of the essence, I had to push these terrible thoughts from my mind. What should I do now? To go back meant certain death. How could I go forward with no clothes on? These men would surely denounce me. Then on the ground I saw an old potato sack. I picked it up and ripped three holes in it, one for my head and two for my arms. I pulled it on and as I felt that rough, cold, clammy material moving down over my skin I said to myself,
"Josef, what are you afraid of? If you haven't been killed today, then you never will be killed. Only G-d can take your life from you now. These butchers have had their chance. They have tried and failed!"

I emerged from the forest, walked up to a farm-hand and said,
"Excuse me, who is in charge here?"
He pointed out the manager. I went up to him and asked,

"Would you like to have another pair of hands to work for you? I could use something to eat."

It must have been obvious that I had escaped from somewhere, but he didn't ask any questions. He took me into the house, fed me and gave me a shirt, trousers and shoes and I started to work for him. I spent six to eight weeks working on that farm, but very early one morning the farmer came rushing into the barn where I was asleep in the loft and cried out,

"Josef, you must leave. Get out now! The Germans are making a sweep of the area and I don't even want the smell of you here, otherwise we'll all be killed. I've prepared a parcel of food for you, but be quick!"

He pointed me in the direction of the nearest railway station and I set off, grateful for the unquestioning help the farmer and his family had given me over the last weeks.

When I arrived at the station, a train was just about to depart. I didn't care where it was going, I just wanted to get as far away as possible. I couldn't travel in a wagon for fear of being caught, so I hid between two carriages, balancing myself by straddling the bumpers. Even though this was extremely precarious, I was so exhausted that I fell asleep. I don't know how long I slept or how far we travelled, but I was awoken when the train suddenly jerked to a halt. A railway guard grabbed me by the shoulder and handed me over to an SS officer. I looked around and saw we were in Cracow station.

The SS officer took me to the nearby ghetto. Some of the inmates, those who were strong enough, were hired out to factories and nearby farms as slave labourers. The employers paid wages for the work carried out directly to the SS, who kept the money. Each camp and ghetto worked in a different manner. Here, you received a work permit to leave the ghetto and go to one's designated place of work. One day, I was ordered to join a group and go fruit-picking in an enormous orchard. We were picking apples and pears, and had a real feast, eating one apple, putting the next in the basket!

The following day, I had not been assigned a specific task. As I still had my work permit from the previous day, I decided to try my luck and see if I could escape from the ghetto. When the guard at the gate asked where I was going I just waved my piece of paper at him and he let me through. Unfortunately, although I could speak German I couldn't read it and before long I was stopped by an SS officer who actually read the permit. It had the name of the fruit farm on it and yesterday's date. The permit had only been valid for one day! The SS officer, his gun at my back, marched me into Crakow-Plaszow concentration camp.

This camp had recently been built on the site of a Jewish cemetery. Graves had been desecrated and the headstones broken up and used to make paths. Some of the blocks were allocated according to one's trade. In one barrack you would find watchmakers, in another cobblers, tailors in another. The Germans were fussy about how they looked and relied on the unpaid skills of the inmates to keep them looking smart. There was also plenty of manual work to be carried out by those who were unskilled, particularly as at that time a new railway line was being built from Cracow main railway station right into the camp.

The Commandant, Amon Goeth, was an overweight, ugly-looking brute, physically nothing like the actor who portrayed him in the film, 'Shindler's List'. Spielberg was accurate, however, in his characterisation – Goëth was a psychopath. Every morning he would come out onto the balcony of his house and shoot at anyone he could see. If he didn't kill twenty or thirty people before breakfast it ruined his appetite! He would play games: lining up prisoners close behind each other, he would fire at them to see how many could be killed with a single bullet. During the day, he rode around the camp on a magnificent white horse, his two large dogs following him. He was especially proud of these dogs, which he had trained to kill people by tearing them apart in ten seconds. He refused to allow prisoners to speak to him directly and when he spoke to one of us there was always a guard acting as an intermediary.

When I arrived at the camp, there were inmates on the appel ground[1] waiting for their instructions, and I was put with them. A new block had just been erected and we were told this was to be our accommodation. Once inside, I recognised a man – it was Uncle Jacob, my father's brother-in-law! We were delighted to find one another and he told me his son, Josef, was in another block. My uncle was working on the new railway track and my cousin's job was to fill the gaps under the barracks. Although I too was assigned this task, I worked under a different barrack.

These barracks were built on stilts. The Germans had decided to fill in the gaps with a mixture of stones and concrete to prevent the prisoners hiding underneath. A group of younger inmates, myself included, were put to work mixing concrete and carrying it in buckets over to the

---

[1] Main square of a camp where inmates would line up to be counted.

barracks. One day as I was kneeling down working, I saw a pair of hooves near me. Without thinking, I looked up. There was Goëth astride his beautiful, white horse.

He leaned down and slashed me across the face with his riding crop.
"No-one looks at me!" he snarled, and rode on.

I was lucky. Others had been shot for much less. The kapo[1] was not so forgiving, however. He was afraid that my action could put him in trouble. He came over and said,
"You know that Goëth never speaks to us directly – it's amazing you weren't killed - but don't worry, I'll make sure when you come to work tomorrow you won't return to your barrack again!"

Tomorrow is another day, I thought to myself wryly.

The next day, when volunteers were called for, I was the first to step forward and we were taken to work on the railway. My uncle was toiling a few yards away and gradually I managed to nudge my way towards him. The work was extremely arduous, especially as we were existing on meagre rations. The guards were patrolling with Alsatian dogs straining on their loose leashes, lashing out at the prisoners whilst encouraging the dogs to pull at our flesh. Many people died daily, but the guards were playing games - there would be plenty more 'volunteers' to replace them.

---

[1] Kapos were prisoners selected by the Germans to supervise the work groups.

The German officers were enjoying an easy life – drinking, smoking, relaxing, and strutting around in the immaculate uniforms which the inmates had to keep up to scratch. They were giving their orders to the guards, who were mostly Polish men in German uniform. Not only were these Poles carrying out the orders of their superiors but they were doing so with relish.

After five days, I was totally exhausted. My uncle had taken a terrible beating that day, and I knew I would not last much longer, so the following day I 'volunteered' for other work. I was sent to join a group who were digging a huge hole. It was near the boundaries of the camp. We had no idea what the hole was for and, as I wasn't there when it was completed, I do not know to this day. But I did find myself working alongside my cousin Josef. We were exhausted and weak from our daily toil and organised ourselves by relaxing our pace of work when the guards moved away. We put a look-out on the rim of the dig to keep watch for the guards. As they approached, the look-out would call down to us 'avodah gadolah'[1] and we would step up the pace. The Polish guards soon came to understand our warnings and would mockingly call them out to us as they neared the worksite.

An underground movement existed within the camp. Groups of saboteurs were organised, whose aim was to make life as difficult as possible for the Germans. They also circulated 'camp zlotys' as a means of barter. If one was caught with them, however, it meant certain death. Somehow I managed to obtain some zlotys. Josef had told me that our cousin, Pepi, was in the women's section of

---

[1] Hebrew for 'work hard'.

the camp, separated from us by a high barbed-wire fence. Anxious to see her, I went to the wire and quietly called her name. Suddenly, someone answered.

"I'm here!" she cried. She was very excited to see me and we exchanged a few furtive words. But we only had moments.

"Do you need anything?" I asked.

"Only bread," she answered.

I told her to come back to the same spot when darkness fell and I would see what I could do. I knew one of the men in the bakery and, with my zlotys, managed to buy a small loaf and smuggle it away. When it was dark, Pepi was waiting at the wire as arranged and I tossed it over to her.

The next day I told Josef of my escapade and how pleased I was to have seen Pepi. While we were talking, they called for 'volunteers' to collect our food. This was not a regular daily occurance, so we all volunteered! Food consisted of three medium-sized metal barrels containing cabbage soup to be shared amongst those working at the hole – about fifty of us. Josef and I, along with four others, were chosen. Each barrel was carried by two people on two rods that fitted under the handles. Hoping to have selected the thickest soup, we carried it back to our work party. We dished it out and finally sat down to have ours. As we looked into our mugs, the contents appeared to have a life of their own. Maggots were wriggling around! We glanced about us. Nobody said anything - everyone was eating the soup. We pushed the worms to one side of the mug and drank from the other. Like many of our 'meals', this one was taken in complete silence.

Many years later, when I was visiting Josef in Israel, we were talking about those terrible times. We had been re-united for the first time in 1974, when I had taken my wife and family to Israel the year of my son Mark's Bar Mitzvah. Josef started talking about the guards in Cracow-Plaszow, especially the one who used to call out 'avodah gadolah!'

"And what about the coffee? We always believed it was made of roasted sawdust!"

Then he recalled the 'food' we were given.

"There were worms wriggling about on the top of the soup. I used to hold them back with my hand, but some people just used to drink them down."

"Yossel," I reminded him. "I was there with you, don't you remember?"

He had a faraway look in his eyes.

"Yes," he said, "I had just forgotten. No wonder seeing you here has brought these memories back."

Nobody could ever understand the inner joy we each felt sitting at peace in a homely environment with our wives and children around us. After that visit, we tried to go to Israel every year, always visiting what family I had left.

In late 1942, as soon as the railway track was ready, a 'selection' was made. We were tightly packed into cattle wagons. The doors were locked once again and we had no food, no water, no sanitation and insufficient air. The stench became horrifying. People were taken ill and many died. After four days of waiting, another train, already filled with prisoners, was hooked onto ours and we started our journey. It was not long before the train stopped. The front wagons had pulled up at a platform.

The people inside had clearly come directly from their homes, still wearing their own clothes and clutching their suitcases and other possessions. We, on the other hand, were seasoned prisoners wearing our blue-and-white striped camp uniform. We watched through the slits in our wagons as the guards ordered the people down onto the platform and told them to leave their belongings.

"Don't worry about your luggage," they said. "Make sure the suitcases are properly marked with your name and we will bring them to you."

The men, women and children were marched away and disappeared down some steps. They had gone straight to the gas chambers. We were in Auschwitz.

The doors of our wagons were unlocked. Our section of the train had not stopped at a platform so we had to jump down. As always, everything had to be done in double quick time. There was screaming and shouting, guards lashing out and beating anyone who could not get out of the way. Dogs on the end of short leads were barking and jumping up at the new arrivals, viciously biting many of them. I saw old people, ill people, people so weak that they were almost dead, come tumbling out of the wagons when the doors were opened. Then I saw a baby being born as its mother was pushed out onto the ground. An SS guard grabbed the baby, cut the cord and threw it unceremoniously to one side, like so much rubbish. He pushed the distraught mother to where a smartly dressed Commandant was deciding who was to live and who was to die. Waving his riding crop, he indicated 'links oder rechts'[1] with a flick of the wrist in a most casual, almost

---

[1] 'left or right'

63

bored way. Those he sent to the left (over 70 percent) went immediately to the gas chambers, those to the right had been selected, either to work or for experimentation. It was Dr Mengele.

Dr Josef Mengele was very aristocratic in stature. All the SS were in awe of him and admired him greatly. He became known as the 'Angel of Death' since few of the thousands of prisoners he selected for his hideous experiments survived. Mengele subjected his victims to clinical examinations, blood tests and anthropological measurements before injecting them with various substances, dripping chemicals in their eyes, apparently in an effort to modify their colour. All his experiments were carried out without anaesthetic.

When I was reunited with two of my surviving sisters in 1954, I discovered that one of them, Rachel, had been subjected to his attention, but she was one of the 'lucky' ones: Rachel survived.

FROM CAMP TO CAMP

How could people behave in such unbelievably inhuman ways? It was clear that the speaker was holding back, trying to temper the horrific events etched into his memory and choosing his words carefully to address these youngsters. Yet the images would be forever burned into their minds – the newborn baby wrenched from its mother, a life lost at its very inception, the hard labour endured by the young boy, who only had worm-ridden soup for nourishment, the lonely orphan fighting each day for his existence, all the while trying to push away the sight of his mother and family falling lifelessly into the pit.

I felt hot tears burning in my eyes and blinked hard to hold them back. The pupils had no such restraint, and some were crying quite openly.

Dr Mengele! Now there was a name that one recognised. In May 1943, after recovering from wounds sustained on the Eastern Front as a result of which he was awarded the Iron Cross, Mengele had been declared medically unfit for combat and appointed a Commandant of Auschwitz. There he was able to continue the research he had been doing before the outbreak of the war at the University of Frankfurt, and was given extra grants to do so. He was said to have been omnipresent at Auschwitz, doing selection duty even when it was not his turn, so eager was he not to miss any potential 'object' for research. The guards were told to look out for anyone, particularly children, with a visible abnormality, be they giants, dwarfs, if they had a cleft palate, and especially twins. These children were separated from the others and given a series of numbers on their arm, distinct from the rest. They were housed separately and endured daily blood tests. Blood transfusions would be given from a twin to his sibling and the effects monitored. Diseases, such as typhus or TB, would be injected into a twin and, after the twin had succumbed to the disease, both twins would be killed and their bodies examined by the pathologist to see the changes wrought by the disease. Limbs were amputated, organs and tissue removed. Finally, death was induced in the form of a chloroform injection administered straight into the heart of the victim. Of around 3,000 children (1,500 sets of twins) selected for these experiments, only about 200 were alive when Auschwitz was liberated by the Soviets on 27th January 1945.

After the war, the Frankfurt Court charged him 'in absentia' with "hideous crimes" against humanity, committed "wilfully and with bloodlust". They listed selections, lethal injections, shootings, beatings and other forms of deliberate killing. Mengele had managed to flee to South America, however, where he would boast of his experiments, and was never brought to justice.

Josef continued.

In a way, you could say that Mengele saved my life because he sent me to the right and I lived. We were marched off to a block where we were told to undress, and those amongst us who were barbers were ordered to cut off our hair. Then we were ordered to walk to the concrete building "to shower", so they said. But those going into the gas chambers had also been told they were going to the showers and Zyklon B gas had poured out of the ceiling – not water. Naked and fearful, we made our way there, ankle-deep in mud after some heavy rainfall. Were we really going to have a shower?

On the way, I suddenly realised to my amazement that I still had my shoes on.
"Well," I said to myself, "while I still have my shoes, I won't be killed."
Don't ask me to explain the logic in that thought! Was it the optimism of a thirteen-year-old?

We were crowded into the shower room and, overcome by cold and fear, some broke down and cried. Then, to our utter amazement and relief, cold water rained down on us. The shower was cursory and afterwards we were given striped uniforms and marched back to our blocks.

In Auschwitz the 'Blockältesters'[1] were German criminals. Many were murderers who had been offered a pardon in return for doing this work, and they did so with gusto. One was heard boasting about how he had killed his own parents.

---

[1] People in charge of keeping order in the block.

There were a thousand people to a block and going in was in itself life-threatening. Each barrack had a platform in the centre. The Blockältesters would be standing on the platform with baseball bats in their hands. One had to run the gauntlet every time one went in or out. If you caught the wood you were as good as dead. It was a great game for these Germans.

We were counted every morning and every evening. Why, I don't know. There was nowhere we could have gone. The fence was electrified and we were too weak to have attempted anything anyway. The guards made sure everyone was accounted for, both the living and the dead. First the Ältesters would count us, and then the SS would come and do a recount to make sure there had been no mistake.

After an appel one day, a section of us on the parade ground were ordered to fill waiting lorries and we were taken to a railway station where we were loaded onto open train wagons. From Poland, we travelled through Czechoslovakia and into Germany. Passing under one bridge in Czechoslovakia, we were showered with pieces of bread which the locals were throwing down for us. The Czechs must have been used to seeing wagonloads of prisoners pass through and looking out for the next transport. What a wonderful feeling it gave us to realise that there were still some people out there willing to put themselves at risk for us.

We began to detect a stench of decaying bodies and realised we must be approaching our destination. We had arrived at Dachau.

Here, as in most places, the camp was divided into different sections – work groups, kitchen groups, those dealing with disposal of the dead. In some blocks, inmates were locked up and just left to die. The female German guards, pistols at their hips and Alsatian dogs tugging on their leashes, would check up on these locked barracks daily, counting the dying prisoners where they lay on their bunks. The dead would be removed and disposed of – replacing them was never a problem. Initially, I worked in the kitchen, but I never stood still, always volunteering, believing that as long as I worked, although I may be beaten, I would stay alive.

Once, when I stepped forward to volunteer, I found myself removing bodies from outside the blocks when they were thrown out, and putting them on a wooden wagon that, when filled, we pulled over and added to a mound of other dead. Another time, I worked on the delousing team, collecting clothes together and burning them. I was always on the go. If you stopped someone noticed and you were as good as dead. All around me people were dying. I was living a nightmare.

One day, a man who was taking a terrible beating from an SS officer was begging for his life. The officer looked down at him disdainfully and sneered,
"Why do you want to live, you fool – you're better off dead! And even if you do survive, no-one will believe what you tell them!"
He was right – if any of us got out of here, who indeed would believe us? But I was determined to keep the

promise I had made to my father and somehow or other I was going to survive.

People were being rounded up. I didn't give it a second thought and contrived to join with the others filing onto the transport, which took us on a long journey to Bergen-Belsen in the north of Germany.

Belsen had a completely different set-up to anywhere I had been before. It was huge and covered a vast area. There were countless sections within the camp. There were English, American, Russian and other prisoners-of-war, each nationality in a separate section. There were political prisoners and many other types of prisoner, each type in their own separate block. There were blocks of Jewish inmates who were used as a commodity with which to barter. The Germans hoped to exchange them either for their own prisoners-of-war from other countries, or for military hardware. Those inmates were even allowed Red Cross parcels and their general living conditions were better then I had seen before. Despite that, once a week, the guards would enter the special Jewish blocks, calling out people by name, and removing them. Each week, there were new arrivals, and each week removals. Yet, in Belsen, too, there were sections where people were locked in their barracks, never seeing the light of day, and left to die.

There was no work in Belsen and people just walked about aimlessly. In the women's section, most just starved to death. When we had arrived at the camp, the stench had been overwhelming, but I was used to it by now. Because there was no work to do, the Germans invented 'jobs'. Someone would be put in charge of 'bed making' in the barracks, making sure – with a ruler – that the bunk was completely smooth and level once the blanket had been tucked in. Luckily, I found myself working in the kitchen once more. The prisoners-of-war had to be fed, so I was peeling potatoes and carrots and generally helping out. In this way, I had enough to eat while I was there, and managed to remain at that job until I left the camp.

The SS officers lived just outside the camp perimeter with their families. I could never understand how they could bring up their offspring under such conditions. The smell permeated the air for miles around. What kind of people were they? They would give guns to their own children, and tell them to take pot-shots at the Jews. These children, my age, would shout,
"Look what I've done, Daddy, look what I've done – I've killed a bastard Jew!"
Given half a chance, I would have torn them apart.

That winter, I was put on a transport to Gross Rosen. This camp was near Striegau in Lower Silesia and had been established in August 1940. From early 1942 its gas chambers were in operation, exterminating prisoners from all over Germany. When my transport arrived, overcrowding was so severe that we were given canvas tents to sleep in. Even in the tents there was insufficient space and we slept leaning on one another as a litter of puppies might snuggle up to their mother.

There were numerous satellite camps in the vicinity, and shortly after our arrival I was sent to one of them, Bolkenhain, to work. This camp had been set up in open fields on the outskirts of Bolkenhain. Barracks, kitchens, an entire camp had been erected, and was surrounded by electrified fencing.

BOLKENHAIN

Here, to our amazement, we were called by our names, whereas previously we had been referred to by number. Soon after our arrival, my group was ordered to assemble near the lorries. We were all terrified and, although we had been allocated our blocks and been assured we were coming back, we feared we would be killed. Some men helped me and three other boys hide down a manhole in a washroom. The others climbed on the lorries and departed. We waited several hours until we thought it was night-time, but when we tried to clamber out discovered that we were too weak to lift the manhole cover and so we had to stay where we were and hope someone would be able to release us.

Hours passed and, as we were in total darkness, we could not tell how much time was passing. We had no food or drink and thought we were going to die. After what seemed like an eternity we heard voices, and the same people who had helped us move the manhole covers and hide came to find us and pulled us out. They told us that we had been down there for four days and nights, and that the reason for the transport was to have numbers tattooed on their arms. When the roll-call was taken that

73

night it was by numbers - and we had none! When the guards realised what had happened, we were severely punished. They wanted to know how and where we had hidden, and who had helped us. Of course, we wouldn't tell them, and so the beatings went on for days.

Eventually, the four of us were marched out of the camp at the head of a column of prisoners. We arrived at a factory and, together with about twenty of the youngsters in the group, we were sent into an untidy room full of machinery parts. The room had glass windows all around, and we could see other prisoners working in the factory. After a while, I realised that there were a lot of bicycle parts lying around and, as I used to have a bicycle of my own, I thought it would be a good idea to see if we had enough bits and pieces to put together a whole bicycle. I found it hard to stand there doing nothing, so I gestured to my three friends and we set to work. By midday, a bicycle was beginning to come together and, after we had been given a bowl of soup, we continued with our task.

When evening fell, the four of us were again put at the front of the column and marched back. It was a long way to Bolkenhain camp, and anyone who fell behind was shot - no-one bothered to collect the bodies, just kicking them to the side of the road. The next day, we were taken back to the factory, which was called 'VDM' – 'Vereinigte Deutsche Metalwerke' - which manufactured aircraft parts and explosives. There, an Italian prisoner-of-war who was an engineer by profession instructed us on a set of machinery in one section of the factory. Throughout the day, he took us from machine to machine and showed us how each job was done. At the end of the day, he told

74

me that he was putting me in charge of the light engineering section, which was made up of young boys, eleven to sixteen years old. My responsibility was to check that the work was carried out satisfactorily and all the parts were in working order. I was told that I had been put in charge because the guards had seen how I had organised my friends to build the bicycle out of parts.

I was given metal discs, which I carried on a ring pinned onto my jacket. Each disc had my number on it and I would exchange these for parts as and when required. In this way, the factory kept a precise record of who had taken each part. I was also in charge of taking broken aircraft parts to an oven which heated the metal and softened it so we could remove the screws, which were then reused. Even the oven had more than one use, and we used it for delousing. Now and again, when it was possible, I would gather some of the boys' clothes and take them to the ovens. There, I would heat them carefully, killing the lice whilst not burning the clothes, and then shake them vigorously so the lice fell out onto the floor.

Lice were a constant problem in every camp and Bolkenhain had its own way of dealing with it. Every two weeks, we would have to strip and stand in the appel quad whilst our clothes were deloused by other prisoners. By heating and eliminating many lice in the factory ovens, we often shortened the time we had to stand naked and wait for our clothes. One day, after we had walked back to the camp from our day-shift at the factory, we were told to strip for delousing. It was a bitterly cold night and snow was thick on the ground. We had been ordered to stand in rows of five, but as the night wore on we huddled closer together for some warmth. In the early hours of the morning, our clothes were returned to us and we were ordered to return to the factory for our next shift. We had not been able to sit down all night and had received no food or water. Those who had been standing around the edge of our huddled pack had succumbed to the elements and frozen to death where they stood.

In Bolkenhain, as in all camps, there were 'Blockältesters', 'Lagerältesters' and a 'Laufer'[1]. Here, however, these were Jewish prisoners given a certain responsibility in exchange for favours. Whereas the 'Blockältester' was in charge of a barrack, the 'Lagerältesters' were charged with keeping order throughout the camp. The 'Laufer' in our camp was a tall, strapping youth called Motek who ran messages between the SS and the Lagerältesters. Motek was unbelievably sadistic and had immense influence and power.

One day he tormented me until eventually I said to him, "Motek, I know you are powerful in the camp and you are stronger than me, but if you kill me I promise I will come back and haunt you and make you wish you had never been born. You will suffer such a slow death that my name and my face will be imprinted on your mind until you die." Somehow, I put the fear of death into him and he left me alone. This did not stop him showing the SS he could be just as brutal as they themselves were. He was even prepared to kill prisoners himself to show the SS he was just like them.

---

[1] A messenger boy.

The factory, too, was overseen by SS guards who were constantly on patrol, walking up and down between the machines. If anyone fell asleep they were shot. I developed a good relationship with the Commandant of the factory as the output in our section was of an excellent standard and, after a few weeks, persuaded him to allow me to collect some leftovers from SS meals for myself and my fellow workers.

In late 1944, after I had been in Bolkenhain for about a year, someone in the factory sidled up to me and said,
"Slow down Joe, not a lot of work is coming in and we don't know what's going to happen. If we run out of work, the Germans might kill us all!"
I explained to him that I was on a time and motion study and if I didn't fulfil my quota of finished parts, my section would be disposed of in any event. Nothing more was said, but a fortnight later, the same person approached me with another request. He was part of the underground movement in the factory, of which I knew nothing, and he told me they were trying to sabotage the factory. This time, I had to listen and follow instructions - I was dead if I did, and dead if I didn't, he told me.

Hand grenades, bullets and bombs were made at the other end of the floor where I worked. The explosive material used was measured out at the start of each shift and whatever was over at the end of the shift would be sent down a chute to the floor below and weighed. There was a chute in my section and we also sent our finished work down to the lower level to be checked.

The activist explained he was going to smuggle a hand grenade over to me and I was to send it down the chute. I was worried about the boys in my section and told him so.

"You organise it so that your boys are in the toilet," he said. "Pull the pin and send the grenade down. Then you go and join them. I'll be back in an hour."

Then he was gone.

When the guard moved away from us for a moment, I sent a whispered message around my section that at my signal they were all to go to the toilet and stay there for a while. It was much too risky to tell them why – the less they knew, the better for them. In any case, they would soon know what it was all about!

The activist returned with the hand grenade which he passed to me, and disappeared. At my signal, the group moved away. I pulled the pin, dropped the grenade down the chute and walked as quickly as I dared towards the toilets. Before I reached them, however, there was a loud explosion. What I didn't know was that the chute divided between the floors and went in two directions. The grenade had lodged between the floors at the intersection, causing damage not only below, but also to our floor and especially where we had been working. Several people were killed and injured on the floors below, but no-one was hurt on our floor until the guards came in firing their guns and screaming at us –

"Who did this? Who's the culprit?"

They were shooting randomly and I was sure we would all be killed. I ran forward and shouted,

"Stop! It was me, I did it!"

The Commandant ordered the shooting to cease. He stormed over to me and said incredulously,

"What do you mean, you did it? I don't believe you!"

What he really meant was that he didn't want to believe me. Since I had been at the factory, we had developed an unusually friendly relationship. Now here I was telling him I had 'betrayed' him. I was sent back to the camp and put into a room in the punishment block. Then the interrogation started.

"Why did you do it?"

"Where did the explosives come from?"

I told them I had done it alone, and to prove it I would show them how. But they didn't believe me, they just wanted to know who had put me up to it. As I wouldn't tell, the torture started. The questions and the beatings were constant. They put needles under my fingernails and gave me electric shocks. My feet were whipped till they were raw and bleeding, and still they beat me. Eventually, I decided that instead of screaming with the pain I would laugh, and so the more they hurt me the more I laughed, until they concluded that I had gone completely mad.

They decided that it was a waste of time beating me any more and left me alone. I was to go to Gross Rosen where I would be hung as an example to anyone else who was thinking of causing trouble.

ESCAPE

At Gross Rosen, I was put into a tiny cell, so small that it was almost impossible to lie down. I had been informed that the following morning I would be publicly hung, but by that time my mental and physical state was such that all I could think of was sleep. Eventually, I closed my eyes, and in my sleep my mother came to me. I knew that she was dead even in my dreams, but still, there she was. My mother was a tall woman, and I wondered how it was that she managed to squeeze into the cell with me. She shook me awake.

"Josef," she said firmly, "your time is not up yet. Don't say anything, just listen. If you look down you will see a small piece of paper on the floor. Wet it with your saliva and put it against the window at the top of your cell. The glass will come away with the paper. Squeeze out of the window, climb down and, a few feet away to the right, you will find a place where you can crawl under the wire and escape."

When I woke up, I looked round for my mother. Of course she wasn't there, but I felt rested now and, miraculously, I felt strength surging through my body and all the pain from the torture I had undergone seemed to disappear. I

Josef's mother, Frieda, with her two eldest daughters, Rivka (left) and Frimid (right) about 1916.

Josef's parents Frieda and Lazar 1939/40.

*From the top: Josef's younger sister Priva, his niece and four nephews
Avraham and Avigdor (children of Rivka), Ezra (Frimid's son)
and Nachala and Srulick (children of Leah).*

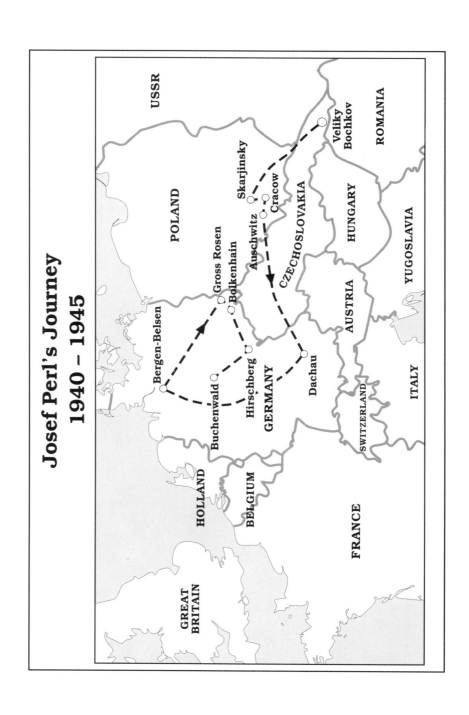

Josef Perl's Journey
1940 – 1945

USSR

POLAND

ROMANIA

Veliky
Bochkov

Skarjinsky

Cracow

Auschwitz

HUNGARY

Gross Rosen

Bolkenhain

CZECHOSLOVAKIA

Bergen-Belsen

AUSTRIA

YUGOSLAVIA

Buchenwald

Hirschberg

Dachau

GERMANY

ITALY

SWITZERLAND

HOLLAND

BELGIUM

FRANCE

GREAT
BRITAIN

In Buchenwald after Liberation, wearing jacket over striped camp uniform.

A.E.F. D.P. REGISTRATION RECORD

Original ☑ Duplicate ☐

For coding purposes

A.	B.	C.	D.	E.	F.	G.	H.	I.	J.

(1) REGISTRATION Nº

(2) Family Name: *Perl*   Other Given Names: *Josef*

(3) Sex: M. ☑ F. ☐

(4) Marital Status: Single ☑ Married ☐ Widowed ☐ Divorced ☐

(5) Claimed Nationality: *Č.S.R. 1000/Harg. rus*

(6) Birthdate: *27. 4. 1930* Birthplace: *Velky Bočko* Province: *Raehovo* Country: *Podko. Rus*

(7) Religion (Optional): *žid*

(8) Number of Accompanying Family Members: *4*

(9) Number of Dependents: ./.

(10) Full Name of Father: *Perl Lazar*

(11) Full Maiden Name of Mother: *Leboričová Frida*

(12) DESIRED DESTINATION

City or Village: *Velky Bočko* Province: *Raehovo* Country: *Podko. Rus*

(13) LAST PERMANENT RESIDENCE OR RESIDENCE JANUARY 1, 1938.

City or Village: *Velky Bočko* Province: *Raehovo* Country: *Podko. Rus*

(14) Usual Trade, Occupation or Profession: *Zámečnický*

(15) Performed in What Kind of Establishment

(16) Other Trades or Occupations

a. *Maď. ezen.* b. *gour. hovor.* c.

(17) Languages Spoken in Order of Fluency

(18) Do You Claim to be a Prisoner of War Yes ☐ No ☐

(19) Amount and Kind of Currency in your Possession ./.

(20) Signature of Registrant: *Perl Józseh*

(21) Signature of Registrar: *Mlada Zorosl.* Date: *11.5. 1945*

(22) Destination or Reception Center:

Assembly Center No.

(23) Code for Issue

Name or Number													City or Village			Province				Country				
1	2	3	4	5	6	7	8	9	10	11	12	13	14	15	16	17	18	19	20	21	22	23	24	25	26	27	28

(24) REMARKS

DR-2

16-30781-1

Displaced person's registration certificate dated 11.5.1945, Josef's only form of identification.

Josef Perl's Journey. Liberation - 11th April 1945 to arriving in London 11th June 1946

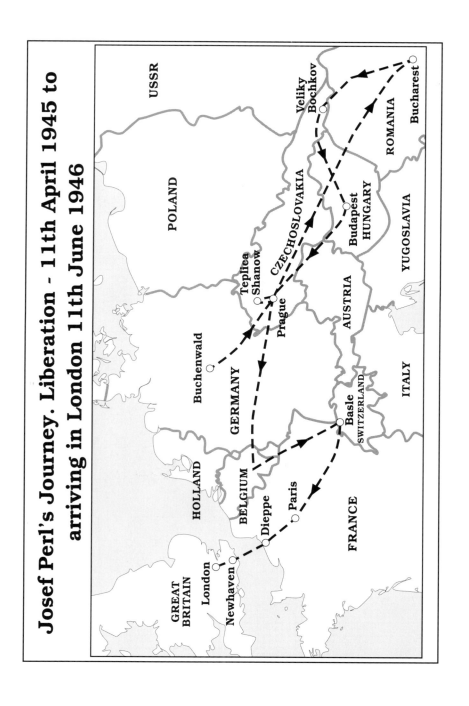

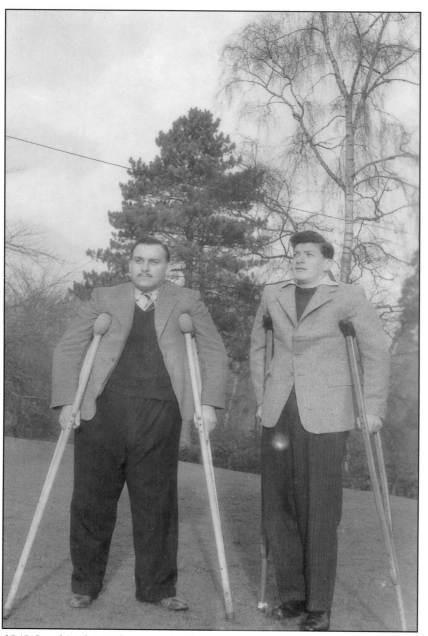

1949 Josef (right) in the grounds of Morland Hall Hospital before his operation.

Sylvia and Josef's wedding in Brighton, 27 November 1955.

Budapest, May 1966. Josef is reunited with his father after 26 years.

May 1966 reunion. Left to right: Rachel, Deborah, Josef, Lazar, Sara.

Sara and Rachel in Bournemouth for the rededication of the family scroll, October 1983.

Bournemouth 1991, Frances's wedding day. At home before the ceremony.

Frances with husband Albert and Benjamin and Ella, 1998.

Josef celebrates his Bar Mitzvah on his 60th birthday; son Mark (29) at his side.

Sylvia and Josef at 'Difference Day,' Calthorpe Park School, 1998.

could hear her voice echoing in my mind and, following her instructions, climbed out of the cell, wriggled beneath the electric wire and ran into the snow-covered forest. Eventually, as day was dawning, I came across the carcass of a dead horse, and I was so hungry that I tried to eat some of the rotting flesh. Suddenly I saw an SS officer approaching. I looked around. I was on the top of a hill. I knew that he had recognised my camp uniform when a shot rang out. I immediately jumped downwards and rolled to the bottom of the hill. As I lay on the snow-covered ground, he fired another three shots at me. One missed, one went straight through my left leg and the other lodged itself in my left knee. The SS officer looked down and, seeing me lying motionless in a sea of bloodstained snow, assumed I was dead. Too lazy to climb down and check, he moved off, leaving me weak and wounded in the snow.

Some time passed, and in the still of the night I realised I could hear voices in the distance. I pulled myself up and saw a group of prisoners being marched along a nearby road. I hobbled over and lay down by the roadside, pretending I was dead. I watched to see where the guards were marching and, when I saw an opportunity, stood up and stepped into line with one of the prisoners. "Who are you?" he asked. "What are you doing here?" He was helping another man, who had become too weak to walk unaided. This man was in a terrible condition and died soon after I joined the line. In the darkness, I exchanged my bloodstained clothes for his, discarding my trousers with their bullet holes and acquiring that person's number, which was sewn onto his jacket. While doing this, I had fallen to the rear of the column. This was always a dangerous place to be, as anyone unable to keep up was automatically shot, so I moved forwards as quickly as I could.

We were marched back into Bolkenhain! When we arrived, it was clear that the camp was being emptied and the Germans were preparing to evacuate the whole camp. The old and the weak had been shot, and were being buried in mass graves under the lookout posts. Wagons were being loaded with provisions to sustain the guards and officers during the journey. We, the prisoners, were to be the 'horses' pulling the wagons. Desperate for food, I saw an opportunity and stealthily stole half a loaf of bread. Fearful of being recognised by the guards or the inmates, I ran into the nearest hut to hide. As I did so, a siren blew, telling us there was an air raid and we should lie face down on the ground outside our huts. I had no choice but to conceal the bread underneath one of the mattresses and then run outside again to lie with the others. When the 'all clear' siren was sounded, I went back to find my bread, but it had disappeared. What could I do? I could hardly report it! All I could do was fall in with the others on the death march.

ON TO HIRSCHBERG

It was the end of 1944 and things were going really badly for the Germans. Although they were coming to realise that they could not win the war, they were determined to continue slaughtering as many of us as they could before it ended. The killing machine which they had set up, the gas chambers and ovens, were no longer adequate for their needs as they weren't able to kill as many Jews as they wanted. So they kept marching us from camp to camp, on Death March after Death March, so-called because of the thousands upon thousands who died or were shot along the way. To accelerate the extermination, prisoners were made to dig huge pits and thousands were shot into these mass graves.

When we left Bolkenhain, no-one knew where we were going, there seemed to be no plan, we were just marched deeper into Germany as the lands they had been occupying were reclaimed by the Allies. About five thousand of us started out on the march, but those who slowed down or collapsed from weariness were shot or clubbed to death. Conditions were so horrendous that some people deliberately fell behind so they would be killed in order to end it all.

Many of the guards were soldiers who had been called out of retirement from the German army. For them, too, conditions were harsh although they had the benefit of food supplies. Each morning, when we were lined up and counted before setting off again, our numbers had diminished. Many died in their sleep from cold and starvation.

We walked for days and days, sleeping in barns, sawmills or open fields. One person had attached himself to me and, as he became weaker and started to slow down, I tried to encourage him.
"Come on, keep going," I said, adding hopefully, "tomorrow maybe there will be a wagon."
His strength was failing fast and he was clinging on to me as I tried to hold him whilst keeping up with the others. If he had fallen, the guards would immediately have shot him.

Many people tried to run away but they were always found and shot. One night, after two weeks of marching, we stopped at a farm and were directed into the barns. I stumbled in, almost carrying my companion. I felt I couldn't go on any longer, I was so weak, my hands and feet were still raw from the torture I had endured at Bolkenhain and my leg was throbbing with pain. Blood was seeping through relentlessly from my wound, and congealing in frozen lumps on the rags I was using as bandages. These bandages were constantly falling down as of course I did not have the right materials, and so during the march I had to keep holding up the bandages as well as carrying my companion. All I could think of now was resting my exhausted body. I made my way to the back of the barn away from prying eyes and, as I passed those listless bodies lying around, I knew a significant number would not be able to get up in the morning.

It was announced that the farmer, unsolicited, had boiled up some marrow, and invited everyone to take their metal cups and have some of the soup. In their emaciated condition, many didn't even have the strength to go and get their share. I managed to drink two cups of the marrow soup, and then moved around my area of the barn checking who was still alive and who had died, to see where I could take some material which was no longer needed and re-dress my wound. I found some wire, which was more efficient than string. I broke off pieces of it, made a figure of eight, hooked the wire to the bottom of the bandage, and hitched it up to my trousers at the top of my thigh. In this way my bandage stayed in place when I walked. Taking off my lice-infested clothes to replace them with those of a dead person, I noticed that I had patches on my chest and looked in amazement at the lice – even they were huddling together against the bitter cold - and grabbed them in great clumps and threw them onto the ground. I put on two sets of clothes. This had two purposes: the first pair of trousers had wire hooks through them and I needed to cover this up and conceal any blood that might seep through, and the jacket was purely for warmth.

I decided to make a run for it. If I were unsuccessful, and caught before I left the farm, I knew I would be shot there and then but at least, I felt, I would be buried there, rather than dying on a march where I knew I would be abandoned by the wayside. I saw an opportunity, bundled up my old lice-infested clothes and made my getaway. Soon, I heard shots ringing out and dogs barking and realised that others had taken the same decision as I had. I left my bloodstained clothes on the ground as a decoy, and hid further off. The Germans were searching the area with their dogs, but when the dogs bounded up to my abandoned clothes, they sniffed around and, finding no-one, went away. I stayed hidden until nightfall. From my hideaway I could see the guards evacuating the prisoners from the farm and continue on their march, and so I carefully made my way back to look for food. I took three raw eggs, pierced a hole in each end and sucked out the inside. Remembering from home that chickens eat the shells from their eggs, I crumpled them in my hands and replaced them near the chickens to hide all trace of my presence. I then moved on to the cowshed and milked a surprised cow before making my way up into the rafters of a barn. In this manner I hid, resting during the day and stealing food under cover of darkness, regaining some strength. After a week, another worn-out, pitiful group of prisoners arrived to stay overnight at the farm and I decided to slip in amongst them, wherever they were going. After another week of marching, we arrived in Hirschberg.

By this time, Hirschberg was seriously overcrowded and the Germans were at a loss to know what to do with us. We would be marched up and down the appel ground like soldiers, ordered to do exercises and leapfrog, we would be called out at any time of the day or night for roll-calls and be kept there, for hours on end. Often when the SS were called for duty they would not arrive because it was so cold. When we were finally dismissed, it was not uncommon for some people to be left standing, frozen to death while standing to attention.

As the Russians advanced from the East, the Germans decided to evacuate Hirschberg, taking as many of us as they could with them. I assume they intended to use us as hostages, and they thought they would be safer guarding half-dead prisoners than being sent to fight on the Eastern front. They selected those they were going to take with them by making us dig a very long ditch, four feet wide and seven feet deep. When it was finished we had to run and jump over it. Those who managed the jump successfully lived, those who didn't fell into the ditch and were shot.

When my turn came I started to run, forcing the pain in my leg to the back of my mind. As I ran, I could hear the person behind me breathing heavily and knew that he wouldn't make it. I jumped with all my strength and, as I landed, I looked over my shoulder and saw him start to slide downwards. Instinctively I grabbed hold and pulled him up just as an SS started firing his gun. Amazingly, he missed both of us and we ran to hide amongst those who were already safe. I was still alive and determined to remain so despite my wounds.

BUCHENWALD and LIBERATION

Those of us who had successfully managed the jump set off yet again. After a few days of marching and sleeping in the open, we stopped at a sawmill overnight. The next morning we were marched to a nearby railway station and put into open cattle trucks. It was bitterly cold and we were packed in more tightly than any cattle would have been. We were shunted backwards and forwards for days as no-one in authority could decide what to do with us. As people succumbed to exhaustion and starvation, the guards threw the bodies over the sides of the trucks. After many days had passed, there were only four of us alive in my wagon, and we had survived by building an igloo-shaped shelter out of the bodies of those who had died. During that time, I lost count of how many people asked me to say Kaddish[1] for them, or how many candles I promised to light. I do know that today I will be going to my synagogue, as I do most evenings, to recite Kaddish.

When our train journey finally came to an end and we were lined up and counted, there were only 178 of us left. I spotted a familiar face some distance away and was

---

[1] Prayer recited for the dead.

amazed to see the companion who had been with me on the march from Bolkenhain. He looked close to death and together we stumbled into Buchenwald. The weakest amongst us were immediately taken away and disposed of, while those who could still walk a little were taken to the showers and given other uniforms. I helped my friend into the shower room, propped him up in a corner, had my shower, collected my uniform and was too drained to think about him any more. I have to admit that in my own struggle to survive, only rarely in the years that followed did I give him another thought. We were taken to Block Number 56 where we were to sleep, and next morning we were given so-called coffee for our breakfast.

Though I would help someone if I could, I needed to stay as independent as possible, never making friends or relying on anybody. We were all very preoccupied with our own survival. In any case, having a friend would most probably mean losing a friend, and that's hard to bear. Each loss takes a part of you and one could so easily descend into a mental abyss from which it would be difficult to return.

Nevertheless, there was a man lying near me who had been severely beaten up and had lost all his teeth. He beckoned me over and asked my name. When I told him, he held out his hand and pressed his food ration disc into my palm. He begged me to take it and smuggle back his bread ration for him, in return for which I could have his soup, as it was not possible to bring this back from the canteen.

Underneath my bunk, another man overheard this exchange and asked if I could do the same for him. I hesitated – if the canteen workers saw me too often they would become suspicious – and it was decided that I would help them out on alternate days. The latter prisoner was an older man, by now chronically weakened by years of malnutrition and mistreatment. After a few days, when I offered him his portion he did not even have the strength to chew it. Can you imagine that, you cannot even make your mouth work? Trying to encourage him, I said,
"Come along, eat! The war is nearly over. We have managed to beat them so far, you mustn't give up now!"
To make eating easier for him, I chewed the bread to soften it and then put it in his mouth. After a few minutes, I realised he wasn't swallowing any more. Whilst I was encouraging him he had simply stopped living. It is impossible to convey to you, who have grown up in a world where food is taken for granted, the pain, yes, the tearing pain of real hunger, and its ultimate consequence.

By the time I arrived in Buchenwald, overcrowding in the camp had reached catastrophic proportions, as had the death rate. In fact, SS records show that, during the first three months of 1945, there were 13,056 deaths. People were arriving in vast numbers as the Germans were moving prisoners further into Germany, away from the oncoming Allied forces. Knowing defeat was imminent, the Germans were nonetheless still determined to annihilate as many prisoners as they could. Conditions in the camp in those last few days before Liberation defy belief.

Block 56 became so overcrowded that I was moved, along with five other young boys, to Block 66, one half of which was occupied by Czech and Hungarian boys, and the other half by Polish youngsters. Here, there were no food ration discs and the Blockältester was a Czech man who was in charge of collecting and distributing the food each day. We were no longer allowed beyond the perimeter of the block, which was defined by a low fence.

We had no work in Buchenwald, we just had to lie on our bunks, immobile. There was no purpose to our lives, nothing to busy our minds with except the awful reality of our plight. Lying there, my mind went back to the happy, carefree days I had enjoyed when my family had all been together and we busied ourselves with family parties, preparations for the Sabbath and Holy Days, and all the animals I had so loved to help care for, and especially my own Bondi and Shari.

Bizarrely, despite my leg wounds and my emaciated state, I would sometimes look at a fellow prisoner and think, "Why are you torturing yourself like this? Why are you clinging on to life? What is this life that you want to hang onto it? Death would release you from such suffering!" I couldn't see that they were mirroring my own condition and that my situation was as dire as theirs.

This state of limbo lasted several weeks. Towards the end, the bodies of those who had died weren't even disposed of, they were either just left in piles around the camp, or simply where they had fallen.

Old scores were being settled amongst the prisoners themselves and those who had collaborated with the SS were now paying the price. The underground movement in Buchenwald was highly organised and, when they gleaned information about a new arrival who had been an over-zealous kapo or Blockältester in a previous camp, immediately eliminated them. Camp justice was carried out.

Rumours began to circulate that the underground movement within the camp was arming itself and planning to liberate the camp from within. Although I was unaware of it at the time, they had managed to make petrol bombs, grenades, bayonets, and had also been supplied with weapons smuggled in by the illegal International Military Organisation. The IMO had been formed at the beginning of 1943 with eleven nations represented. When the Americans, who had been in the vicinity of the camp for the last few days, entered Buchenwald late in the afternoon of 11th April 1945, they found that the Buchenwald prisoners had liberated themselves and the camp was being run by the illegal International Camp Committee. Most of the German guards had fled and the only SS still in the camp were those who had been taken prisoner by the ex-prisoners. It was sixteen days before my fifteenth birthday.

Throughout that day, there had been a great feeling of expectation rippling through the camp and I was lying on the ground outside block 66, warming myself in the spring sun and trying to comprehend the events unfolding around me. When I saw the American soldiers, I struggled to sit up and saw them staring in horrified disbelief at the sight that confronted them.

The tempo of the camp suddenly altered and people were hurrying in all directions. The three layers of fine-meshed wire fencing had been pulled down by the arrival of the American tanks, and those inmates who were strong enough were making their way out of the camp, even for a few seconds – they just wanted to be on the other side of that fence and try to absorb the feeling of freedom.

I looked at the Americans with their guns and clean uniforms and I looked down at myself in my filthy rags, wondering,
"Who am I? Where do I belong?"
The sight of the American soldiers and the realisation that our oppression and merciless persecution was at an end gradually imbued my wounded, emaciated body with renewed hope. This in turn gave me strength. Like many others, my immediate desire and instinct was to pass through the destroyed perimeter fencing. Painfully, I struggled to my feet and, after I had managed to procure a gun, limped slowly through the dismantled wire fence. Once outside, I carried on down the hill towards the nearest farm. I was alive, and sustaining myself was now my priority.

I ordered the farmer to kill a chicken for me and took it back to the camp. I found a rusty can, filled it with the fresh water that had been brought in by the Americans, made a fire and boiled it for a few minutes to clean out the tin. I rinsed it out and boiled up another can of water, plucked, cleaned and cut up the chicken and put it in the can to cook. When it was ready, I drank the soup slowly, a little every two hours, frightened to eat too much after so long without food.

Our liberators had arrived at the camp unprepared. The only food they had with them was their own rations. Shocked by what they saw, and in their eagerness to try and alleviate the suffering around them, they plied the inmates with their supplies. Army rations – pork, beans and chocolate - were totally unsuitable and, tragically, many more lives were lost. Not only had the inmates been malnourished, but by now there had been no food or clean water in the camp for a week. Of the 21,000 people who were liberated on that day in April 1945, only about 700 were alive a few weeks later, and I was one of them. General Patton himself, when he came to the camp and saw the conditions said, "My G-d, why didn't we come here earlier? We could have saved more of these people." As it turned out, he and his men literally killed hundreds of us with kindness.

General Patton was so incensed by what he saw in Buchenwald that he went to the nearby town of Weimar, where he instructed the mayor to order his townspeople to go into the camp the next morning and witness for themselves what the German people were responsible for. He had left orders in the camp that the immense task of burying the piles of dead bodies in mass graves was not to commence until the German citizens had marched through.

The next day, these people were brought up the hill and were met at the gate by an interpreter who carefully and in great detail explained what had been going on in the camp. Words were hardly needed, however, the evidence was all around. As they were going back down the hill, a number of Germans in the group found something to laugh about. This so enraged the troop commander who was accompanying them that he turned them around and marched them back through the camp again, much more slowly this time. When they finally marched back to Weimar there was no more laughter, and I learned later that the next day the mayor and his wife had committed suicide.

On 20 April, Winston Churchill sent a Parliamentary delegation to Buchenwald to "find out the truth" about what had gone on. On 14th May they published their report in which they described the camp as *the lowest point of human degradation to which humanity has yet descended.*"

In 1989, a photograph of me, taken soon after Liberation, at fifteen years old, still wearing my blue-and-white camp uniform in Buchenwald, was sent to me from Israel. A fellow prisoner whom I had met in Israel earlier that year had taken it. I have no recollection of him having taken the photograph, but he had been elated to meet up with me in Tel Aviv on the occasion of my niece's wedding. He told my wife he had always treasured the photo because I had saved his life not once, but twice, and had always hoped he would meet me again one day. Although I could not and still do not remember the details of his story, it was a joyful encounter.

Now, do you remember Motek, the sadistic 'laufer' from Bolkenhain? A few days after Liberation, I heard a commotion outside my barrack. I went outside and saw people throwing stones at someone on the ground. I heard a voice call out – "Look, it's Motek!"

I was amazed that he had escaped retribution at the hands of the Underground movement. A non-Jewish man who had previously been working in the kitchens at Bolkenhain had discovered Motek hiding in the corner of a block. A group of people forced him out and began to throw stones at him. Many joined in, some knew of his cruelty - one had lost a brother and father at his hands - but I stood to one side where he could see and hear me. As he lay on the ground, I called out to him,

"Can you hear me Motek? I'm still here, like I said I would be."

He wasn't the only one who died at the hands of his fellow prisoners in those days. Sadly, too few of those who had perpetrated atrocities on their fellow prisoners with such gusto received the punishment they deserved.

For their part, when the American soldiers saw the suffering the Nazis had inflicted on the inmates and how proud they were of having 'done their duty' so thoroughly, they lined some of them up and shot them.

HOME?

I gradually became a little stronger. The Jewish Chaplain of the American forces conducted services and gave emotional support to the Survivors. He especially involved himself with the children, and tried to encourage many of us to travel to America with him, promising to help us start a new life there. He was a gentle man, a wonderful human being, very suited to his vocation as a Rabbi, and we had many conversations, each time ending with his invitation to return with him to his family. I had an overwhelming desire, however, to go home and find out what had happened to the rest of my family.

But who was I? For five years I had been a number, in fact several different numbers, as I had ditched my bloodstained clothes for 'clean' ones. To leave the camp I would need some kind of identity document. I went to the American Commander's office and said I wished to leave and make my way home. I was issued with a Displaced Person's Registration Record stating,
'Perl Josef, born 27/4/30, Veliky Bochkov, Czechoslovakia, son of Frieda and Lazar Perl. Religion - Jew.'

As well as being an identity document, this also enabled me to go to any United Nations Relief and Rehabilitation Agency (UNRRA) centre and have a meal a day.

You cannot begin to imagine how that little piece of paper made me feel. It told the world I was a person, I was a somebody. Standing naked, head shaved, in unbelievably degrading conditions, for five years they had tried to reduce me to a 'nothing'. But I was here, I had survived, I had triumphed over Nazi ideology. They had not won and this document proved it. I had returned to the human race.

It was about this time that two young German farm-workers came into the camp to tell us that four SS were working on a nearby farm, hiding their identity. Eight of us, armed with guns, went to the farm, found them and were marching them back towards the camp when we encountered a Russian officer. He was a tall man with an impressively bushy beard, in full military dress, medals shining. He stopped us and asked if anyone spoke Russian. I answered, and he enquired what we were doing with these four men. I explained to him they were SS from Buchenwald, and we were going to hand them over to the Americans.
"You're wasting your time," he said contemptuously. "They won't do anything. Has your gun got bullets?"
I replied positively. He snatched it from me and, before we realised what was happening, he had shot them, with no hesitation whatsoever. One of the boys observed that, if the Americans found out what he had done, he could be in trouble.

"It doesn't matter," he shrugged.   "We are leaving tomorrow."

My ears pricked up at this. I asked him where they were headed and, on learning they were going to Prague, asked if I could have a lift.
"We're leaving at ten tomorrow morning. If you are here on time, you can come with us."
I made sure I was there in good time the next morning and, when the officer saw me, he called out in Yiddish, "shpring arauf!" – jump up! It was then I realised that the Russian officer was Jewish.

When the lorry arrived in Prague, the officer set me down.
"This is as far as I can take you," he waved.
As the lorry disappeared from view, I found myself surrounded by perhaps ten or twelve local townspeople, all plying me with questions. They had seen me climb down from the Russian lorry and on approaching me had seen the name 'Buchenwald' written on the sleeve of my jacket. They wanted to know where my hometown was, where I was going, if I needed food, money, somewhere to sleep. I felt overwhelmed: I had entered a new type of world, one where people were interested in my welfare, and trying to help if they could.

They took me to a restaurant and, while I was eating, their questions continued until my head was spinning. That evening I stayed in a hotel, but my leg was swollen and throbbing. The next morning, the same people came to see me and accompanied me to the local hospital. When the doctor examined me he advised that, because the bullet was still lodged in my knee, my leg needed to be put in plaster of Paris, and that I should not put any weight on it but use crutches.

The thought of being immobilised for an unknown period was unacceptable to me, as I had resolved to continue my long journey homeward. Reluctantly, the doctor re-dressed my leg and I left the hospital with my new-found friends. They took me to a farm on the outskirts of town, where an elderly couple had a smallholding. They greeted me warmly and unquestioningly and treated me like their own son. I had my own room to sleep in and plenty of warm water in which to bathe.

Prague had become a meeting place for all those who, like myself, were looking for their loved ones. We were drawn together by the suffering we had endured, exchanging news about people we had met, hoping against hope for information about our families and friends from before the war. I learnt that special centres had been set up in Bucharest, Budapest and all the major European cities where 'displaced persons' could stay overnight, eat and be clothed if necessary. The walls were lined with photos of all those who passed through, and visitors would scour these photos trying to see if there was any face they recognised. There were, too, a number of groups operating in Prague, helping people restart their lives in America, Britain and Palestine.

I stayed on the farm for a few weeks, building up my strength. I knew that my mother and some of my sisters were dead but I had no idea about the other members of my family. As for my father, I clung on to the belief that he was still alive. If he were dead, surely I would have known it in my heart? I had to go and look for him. I wanted to go back home.

I went to Prague station where I met up with several boys and girls, all in the same position as I was, all searching for a way home.   The transport system had been completely disrupted, there were no timetables and nobody knew where the trains were going to or how long it would take to get to the end of a journey. Sometimes a train would pull into a station and stay there for days before continuing.   Other times, the stationmaster would announce that the train would go no further at all. Thousands of people whose lives had been disrupted in the war were travelling all over Europe, everyone with his own story, each with a little hope, not knowing where the future would take them.   Our group tried to stay together and we climbed into the first train we saw.

When we stopped at a station, there was always an UNRRA kitchen specifically for us, where we were given bread, soup and a box of 'American breakfast' containing coffee, tea, cigarettes and so on, which we could take with us for the journey.

If we were told a train would be going no further, we would find other means of transport. I travelled by horse and cart, oxen and once even on the handlebars of a kind man's bicycle for some kilometres - any means possible that would help me return to familiar surroundings. Eventually, I found myself on a train whose destination was Bucharest. I was quite excited to go there as I had heard many stories about the large and well-organised Displaced Persons Centre in that city which had been set up by the Jewish Agency. On arrival at the station, men were calling out amongst the crowd asking people to come forward if they wanted a lift, and I joined a small group which was taken by horse and carriage to the Centre. There, I scrutinised the hundreds of photographs, praying to find one I recognised, but without success. I was given a shirt, jacket, trousers and – to my delight – a brand new pair of leather shoes! I stayed at the Centre overnight and, refreshed and feeling smart in my new clothes, I went back to the station where I found other young survivors and together we took the first train headed northwards.

One evening, when it was clear the train was going nowhere for the next few hours, we alighted and went into the village church to sleep. The villagers warned us not to go into the church as it was said to be haunted. Ghosts couldn't scare us! We took in apples, potatoes and other vegetables we found, ate some and stored the rest in a box which we propped open with two sticks. During the night there was a violent storm, wind and rain was whipping around the church and blowing through cracks in the windows and doors. Suddenly, the sticks keeping the lid open became dislodged and the lid crashed down with a vibrating bang, which resonated around the church. All the boys jumped up immediately, guns at the ready – until, sheepishly, we realised what had happened!

We rejoined the train early next morning and, as it wound its slow path through the countryside, a few of my companions alighted at stations near their homes. When the train reached Sighet, I was on familiar ground and left the train, crossing the border bridge, making my way to

Bochkov. I found myself at the station where, five years earlier, I had been a naïve child of ten, exposed for the first time to the horrors to which mankind could descend, peering through the cracks of a cattle wagon at the bodies of murdered friends, while many villagers who were watching those carrying out the atrocities were cheering to see us go.

Here I was once again, old beyond my years. I had seen things no human being should ever see, been through what no human being should ever have to endure, and my mind was full of nightmarish visions with which I would have to live forever. Was anybody ever going to believe the survivors' accounts, would anybody be brave enough to listen? For the next half a century, man hid the truth from himself and no-one did listen. Even the Allied soldiers who were in Europe at that time were unable to talk about their experiences when they returned home. Not only thinking they might not be believed, but also because they themselves were too traumatised by what they had seen.

I struck up a conversation with a group of men standing at the station and one of them offered to give me a lift on his horse and cart as he was going in the direction of my home. It was a glorious, hot summer's day, the surroundings were peaceful and we chatted along the way. Suddenly, my house came into view. Joyfully, I pointed it out to him and asked him to set me down at the end of the street. I felt I was floating down the road, and stopped at the gate to my house full of hope and expectation, my heart pounding, my mind in a whirl, tears of joy rolling down my cheeks. I stepped through onto the garden path and walked up to the front door.

As I approached, the door opened. I recognised the man as one of our Christian neighbours who had worked for my father. He had known my family since before I was born and we had been good friends. But now, seeing me standing there, a wave of shock and hatred spread over his face. He pointed a shotgun at me.
"You are still alive? What do you want?" he shouted angrily.
"This is my home. I want to come in, I'm looking for my family," I pleaded.
"Get out of here. Get out!" he yelled. "This is my house now. Mine and my children's. Get out, there's no-one and nothing for you here."
"I'm so tired," I begged, "please let me at least sleep in the stable for the night."
He aimed his gun at me again.
"Leave now, or I'll finish Hitler's job for him!"

I pulled out my SS pistol and pointed it at him.
"If I go, I'll take you with me."
He laughed disdainfully.
"Get out!" he repeated, gesturing with his shotgun.

Stunned, I lowered my pistol, forced from my home a second time. The door slammed shut. I walked down the garden path and sat down on the grass by the road where I used to play as an innocent child and sobbed and sobbed for all that I had lost.

Since leaving Buchenwald I had fortified myself with the blind belief that when I arrived home everything would be all right. I had made a mistake in that forest, everyone would be at home waiting for me after all, and we could resume our lives once again. That my father would be there I never doubted for one minute. We had made a promise and I knew that he would have made as much of an effort to keep his side of the bargain as I had. And now here I was, sitting outside my own home and the door had been closed in my face. Like countless other survivors, I had no-one in the world with whom to share my name. I was the last of my line.

I learned much later that of the 300 families totalling about 1,700 Jews living in Velicky Bochkov in 1938, only about 50 people survived.

HIGH AND DRY ONCE AGAIN

After the relief of Liberation and the anticipation of reaching home – and perhaps finding a relative there – even this episode had turned into a nightmare. The pupils sat motionless. Like Josef, they had assumed that once at home his life might return to a semblance of normality. The door they had hoped would be thrown open in welcome had been slammed in his face.

And now here he was, a crippled child, sitting on the grass weeping, his heart broken in a way that, hopefully, none of them would ever experience.

After a while, I staggered shakily to my feet. Dazed, I wandered around all the places I remembered, vainly hoping to see a friendly face amongst the locals. But although I recognised many familiar faces of teenagers and their parents, they chose to ignore me. I didn't approach them, fearful of being tormented or rebuffed. Next to my home had been the synagogue. Now it was being used as a warehouse – our place of prayer was no longer needed here: the Jewish population had disappeared. My heart was pounding, my stomach churning and the need to leave became overwhelming. I vowed never to return.

I walked down to the river and crossed the bridge back into Sighet. Here too, I searched fruitlessly for my relatives who had lived there before the war. Wearily, I went to the station and caught the first train to depart, not caring where it was headed, needing to rest, to sleep, to try and absorb and come to terms with this new loss. Most of all, I wanted to distance myself from my shattered past. I do not know how long I was asleep, but I was awoken by the guards calling for everyone to alight as the train would be going no further.

I was not certain where we had stopped and, seeing a group of people walking together, joined them. After a while, we arrived at a bridge connecting Romania and the Russian-controlled part of Hungary. There were hundreds of people milling around the checkpoint. The Russians had begun to restrict movement and had tightened the borders, deploying their soldiers on the Hungarian side of the bridge. The only way to cross the border was by bribing the guards – both the Romanian and the Russian – and the black market was rife. Realising I did not possess anything with which to bribe the guards, I decided amidst the confusion simply to walk across. Slinging my jacket over one shoulder, I stuck the other hand in my trouser pocket and, stomach churning and heart pounding on the inside, strolled up to the bridge whistling as if I had every right to be there. Approaching the checkpoint, I noticed a group of people who were being allowed across the bridge having, presumably, already bribed the Romanian border guard. I had to act quickly, and attached myself to them. Neither the guards nor those who were crossing challenged me and so I continued confidently across the bridge.

I stayed with the group as I heard they were aiming for Budapest, hoping my luck would continue. We walked for three or four hours until we arrived at the checkpoint which separated the Russian-controlled region and Free Hungary. When we were asked to present our papers, the people I had been with were all let through. The only paper I possessed, however, was the one I had been issued with on leaving Buchenwald. This was not acceptable to the guards and, having nothing to bribe them with and despite my protestations, I was refused entry. A man who had observed the heated exchange approached me and said that if I walked through the forest I would inevitably cross the border into Hungary.

I set off, gathering some mushrooms in my handkerchief for sustenance on the way. After walking for about an hour, I found myself surrounded by a group of heavily armed Russian partisans on horseback.

"What are you doing here?" their leader challenged.
"I'm picking mushrooms," I replied, opening my handkerchief.
"Nonsense – no-one comes this far into the forest just to pick mushrooms!"
He noticed the badge on my sleeve saying 'Buchenwald'.
"You're a Jew, aren't you?" he asked.
"Yes, I am," I said defiantly.
"In that case, we'll finish off Hitler's job for him!"

I suddenly went cold and could feel my heart racing. How many more times was my life going to be threatened? Was there ever going to be any peace in the world? Since I had seen the dead being thrown out of wagons on the transports, or shot on death marches, the fear of being left for dead to be devoured by wild animals and not buried was always with me. But I could not allow myself to show my fears now. The leader continued.
"I give you thirty minutes to pray to your G-d!"

With great difficulty I regained my composure.
"What have I done to you," I questioned, "that you should want to kill me?"
"Why shouldn't we kill you?" came the reply. "You Jews killed Jesus!"
"I'm a Jew but so was Jesus. And anyhow, how could I have killed Jesus? I wasn't even around then," I argued, laughing nervously. There was silence for a moment. How was I going to get out of this one! Then an idea came to me.
"I can see that you know your Bible," I continued. "You're just like Jesus - a leader of men. What will your men think of you, their leader, if they see you killing an unarmed boy like me?"
"You Jews, you're always different – you even eat different foods -"
"I'm starving," I interrupted. "I'll eat anything."

He studied me for a moment. Suddenly, he ordered his men to dismount and bizarrely I found myself sitting in a circle with the men eating brown bread, pork and onions, and drinking vodka. The intense fear and tension I had been through now dissipated, I felt the excruciating pain

109

in my leg. The captain saw me wincing and nursing my leg, and asked about it. I made light of my wound, saying I had fallen and hurt myself and he probed no further. After we had eaten, he asked me where I was heading. When I told him I wanted to go to Budapest, he pulled me up onto his horse, and with his men I crossed the border. They set me down at a farm saying that from there I would find my way to Budapest.

I approached some farm workers who pointed me in the direction of the station, where I caught a train to Budapest. On arrival, I headed straight for the Jewish Refugee Centre, searching the walls of photographs and poring over the list of names of those who had passed through. Finding no-one I recognised, I returned to the station the next day and took a train to Prague.

There I met up with some people whom I had met on my travels. They, too, were still looking for surviving members of their families and exchanging news and information with one another. I even met Slomo who, before the war, had been married to my sister Rivka. Knowing that his wife and two little sons had perished, he was now living with a girl who had a young daughter. We had known her before the war as she was related to him by marriage. When, by chance, he had met her after liberation, she was destitute. Two desperate people – one homeless and the other needing someone to care for, to replace his lost family. They were inevitably drawn together and married soon after I left. Thirty years later, I was reunited with Slomo in Israel, when I had a family of my own. His second wife had died but her daughter was living nearby. We spent many happy times together before he passed away.

At the time, it was all each person could do to support themselves and their depleted families, and so I moved on, having heard that a lot of people from my area were in Teplice Shanow. So I set off once again. I felt I had been wandering enough and perhaps now I could settle down and learn a trade. When I arrived in Teplice Shanow, I encountered a man who had a small metal-workshop. I asked if I could work for him, as I had had experience of light engineering when I was in the camps, in return for board and lodging. I learnt his trade – he was a locksmith and also made cooking pots and utensils. I worked for a short while, but by then my leg was giving me so much pain that I went to the hospital to see if anything could be done. I was admitted and underwent tests and x-rays, my leg was put in a plaster cast and I was told not to put any weight on it and given a pair of crutches. A chest x-ray revealed lesions on my lungs and arrangements were made for me to go to a TB sanatorium in Prague.

I spent about five months in the peaceful atmosphere of that sanatorium, through the winter of 1945-46. Gradually my lungs healed and, except for my leg, my general health improved.

Whilst I was recuperating, I was permitted to leave the hospital grounds. Instinctively, I sought out fellow survivors, and we would meet in a Prague café, exchanging stories of home and other news. One day, I heard that a Jewish organisation based in Prague was

111

now trying to trace any displaced Jewish children in order to send them to Canada and America to make a new start. The British Government had also announced that they would admit a maximum of one thousand 'healthy' children up to the age of sixteen.

The same day, I went to the offices of the Jewish Committee for Relief Abroad to put my name on the list. The JCRA told me, however, that as the British were only taking 'healthy' children and I was still hospitalised, I was not eligible. It was absurd - after what we had all been through, none of us could be described as 'healthy'.
"The only way we could assist you," the official added helpfully, "was if you could prove you were in danger."

While I had been in Prague I had been dealing, along with everyone else, on the black market - mainly selling cigarettes, soap and salt - to make a little money. I had contacts with the local police and I called in a favour from one of the policemen, asking him to furnish me with a letter saying I was in danger of being arrested because of my black market activities. I presented the letter to the official I had seen before at the JCRA, expecting to be put onto the next transport to England. To my amazement, he exclaimed in horror,
"This is far too dangerous! If the local authorities get hold of this they will stop helping you - and anyone else!"
I snatched the letter back, tore it into shreds, threw it into the wastepaper basket and asked,
"What letter are you talking about?"
"OK," conceded the official, smiling, "there's no letter. But we know you are ill and we've been ordered to send only fit people. I'll tell you what we'll do. Go to our medical

unit and have some more chest x-rays taken and if they still show signs of TB then maybe we can send you to Switzerland."

The x-rays showed scarring but no sign of any TB.   I presented them to the official.
"Well," I asked, "am I going to Switzerland?"
"No," he said, "your lungs seem to have healed up very well."
I was overcome with rage and could contain myself no longer. I grabbed a large glass inkwell from his desk and hurled it across the room. It hit the wall, smashing into a thousand pieces showering glass and ink everywhere.

"Not fit enough to go to England and not ill enough to go to Switzerland!" I shouted.   "I'll be back tomorrow, whether you like it or not, and my name had better be on that list!"
The official studied this display of anger calmly.
"When you come tomorrow I'll have another doctor here. We'll see what he has to say."

The following day, as he had promised, there were two doctors standing next to the official. Still agitated from the previous day's frustrating exchange, I immediately started to undress. I took off my jacket hastily and threw it down on the floor. I began unbuttoning my shirt and it swiftly joined the jacket. When I started undoing my trousers, one of the doctors, in an effort to pacify me, held up his hands and said,
"That's enough – you don't need to undress any further."
They examined me, listening to my chest and reading my notes.

"Don't worry. You're all right – you can go to England."

I could hardly believe my ears! They hadn't asked me to take my trousers off, so concerned were they with my chest, and no-one had realised that my leg was encased in plaster from hip to ankle! The official advised me to discharge myself from the sanatorium and gave me an address for lodgings where several other youngsters were also living. After a few days we were told to assemble in a hall where we were taken by coach to the airport and put on a plane bound for England.

THE LONG JOURNEY TO ENGLAND

The plane was a converted bomber with bench seats running down the sides. These aircraft had been designed as fighting machines and were cold, noisy and draughty. Soon after take-off, one of the engines was showing signs of failing and so the pilot was forced to divert to a Belgian airfield for repairs. A few minutes later the engine failed completely and the plane lurched to one side. We approached a landing strip and, while coming in to land, the pilot realised the landing gear was not opening. He shouted at us to sit on the floor in a line, herringbone fashion – each person slotted in between the legs of the person behind – and to hold tight. When we landed, we were to jump out as fast as we could and run away from the aircraft in case it blew up. On landing, the bump caused the person in front of me, who had his left elbow over my plaster, to put pressure on my leg which cracked the plaster. The cast dug into my leg and it started to bleed. Whilst everyone was jumping out of the plane and running, my leg slowed me down. Blood was pouring down into my shoe and I was quite a distance from the other children.

The local Jewish community had been alerted that a plane containing children was making an emergency landing, and people were already arriving on the scene to see if they could help. A young couple came forward to greet me and I explained that I couldn't go on because my leg was bleeding, and confided that I couldn't tell anyone, as it would prevent my entry into England.

The lady went back to the relief group, who were already distributing food and drink, to find out what arrangements were being made. She learnt that we were to continue our journey by train as soon as possible. The couple took me back to their home, removed my shoe, cleaned my foot and tightened the plaster with bandages as best they could. They put me to bed, saying they would go and see how the travel arrangements were progressing.

I awoke to find the couple in deep discussion in the kitchen. They told me that the group had already departed for Paris by train.
"Don't worry," my hosts said. "We know people who can arrange things for you. A doctor friend of ours, who works with refugees, will be arriving soon from Switzerland. Stay with us until then and we'll see if he can take you with him as he's going on to Paris and perhaps you will be able to link up with your group again."
When the doctor came he readily agreed to take me, explaining that he would be going to Paris via Switzerland where many survivors were recuperating. I looked in vain around the hospitals and sanatoriums we visited there for a familiar face. After a few weeks, we continued our journey to Paris where he had heard that there was a group of children at Rothschild's château.

On arrival there, I was astonished to see my group, still waiting for transport to England. I approached the person in charge and explained that I had accidentally been left behind in Belgium and had been trying to catch up ever since. He shook his head. Every now and again someone found a relation, or decided not to continue their journey. Whoever didn't arrive for the morning register was removed from the list.

"I'm sorry," he said. "I'm afraid there's nothing I can do. Your name isn't on my sheet any longer - but you can stay with us here for a while if you like."

Before he returned to Belgium, the doctor visited me at the château. I told him how painful my leg was because the cast had been broken, and he took me to a local hospital where the plaster cast was reinforced.

On my return to the château, I discovered that one of the boys was waiting for his uncle to come and collect him, and he had not yet informed the organisers that he was no longer going on to England. Immediately, I sought him out and asked if I could use his name so I could remain in the group.

"Of course, Joe", he replied without hesitation. "And I wish you good luck with it!"

After about six weeks, the Jewish organisation managed to hire a boat and, on 11th June 1946, approximately 120 boys and girls were taken from Dieppe to Newhaven. Upon our arrival in England, we were welcomed by representatives of Jewish organisations and given food and drink. My first experience of English hospitality was tea - with milk! We wondered what this strange drink was, it looked such a

dull colour. Some of us didn't even dare try it and tipped it out. Fresh fruit was also handed round in baskets – apples, plums, pears – but we were particularly fascinated by the long, yellow fruit. What could it be? How do we eat it? We were given a demonstration:
"You peel it like this," smiled the man.
That was the first time I ate a banana!

Meanwhile, the organisers were telling us how to register our arrival.
"We realise many of you may have given false details to enable you to get this far," we were told. "But now we need your true names and ages. There's nothing to be frightened of any more – you're safe here, no-one's going to send you back."

Proudly, I stood in line, and announced myself as "Josef Perl", fourteen months after I had struggled to my feet in Buchenwald and asked myself, "Who am I?"

A LOT OF BANANAS

We were taken by train to London and housed in the Jewish Shelter in Mansel Street in the East End. Only then did I inform the organisers that I desperately needed to go to hospital and have a new plaster cast fitted. They were astonished.

"What do you mean, your leg is in plaster? What's the matter with it? How did you manage to pass a medical?"

There was a flurry of activity, and the next day I was taken to the London Hospital in Whitechapel. The plaster had been stuck to my leg with dried blood for several weeks, and removing it was a difficult and painful task. But after having had to conceal my great discomfort for so long, what a relief it was when a new, more comfortable plaster was finally applied.

A week or so after we arrived at the Shelter, a day trip to Brighton was organised for a group of twenty girls and boys. We were each given half-a-crown pocket money and we set off for the train station. When we arrived, we passed a greengrocer's shop just outside Brighton station. I was amazed at the wide variety of beautiful fruit and vegetables on display and especially marvelled at the bananas. I pointed to them, held out my money, and the

119

greengrocer gave me a huge bunch of bananas in exchange. We all walked down in glorious sunshine to the seafront and strolled along the promenade towards our host's house in Hove, all the time eating the bananas and chatting merrily.

We arrived at a delightful house with a large back garden. While the others were singing, shouting and jumping about playing leapfrog, I sat just inside the house by the French windows, watching them. After a while a woman came in and spoke briskly to me in Yiddish,
"Why aren't you outside enjoying yourself with the others?"
"Listen," I retorted, "if I want to go outside I'll go and if I don't want to - then I won't!"
I had no idea who she was. She was wearing an overall and I supposed her to be a maid, helping to prepare food for us.

When the dinner gong sounded she came back as I had remained sitting in the lounge.
"Why aren't you going in for dinner?" she enquired.
"Because I am full of bananas, and I'm not hungry," I replied ungraciously.

Some time later, I heard a voice. I looked up and saw a smartly dressed lady standing before me. I realised with embarrassment that it was the same person I had spoken to earlier and she was, in fact, our hostess! She brushed aside my apologies and sat down beside me, plying me with questions about my family. It was too painful for me to talk about my past, so I changed the subject and asked about her own family. As the conversation developed, she told me of her son, Balfour, and her daughter, Ruth, who was about my age. There was a huge picture on the wall in the lounge of a young man in uniform and I asked who he was.

"That was my eldest son," she said sadly. "He was killed during the war."

She went on to describe how intelligent, learned, generous and kind-hearted he had been and how he had had a brilliant academic future ahead of him. Tears were running freely down her cheeks.

"Listen," I told her. "You have another son and I'm sure he'll grow up to be a professor and do well. You still have two lovely children who are alive and close to you. Live for them."

By now, the others had finished their dinner and gone back into the garden. The lady asked me if I wanted anything, but I declined, politely this time. It was soon time for us to leave for the station, and as we gathered in the hallway, the lady came over to me.

"You aren't going back to London," she said firmly, "you're staying here!"

"I can't do that, I'm with the group," I replied, surprised.

"It's all right," she assured me. "I've arranged it with London, and you are staying here with us. No arguments."

The couple were Professor and Mrs Jacob Halevy, and they owned and ran Whittingham Jewish College in Brighton. They were both active members of the local Jewish community and worked tirelessly for the Zionist Federation. Mrs Halevy was to become President of Youth Aliyah in Brighton, a committee helping Jewish youngsters emigrate to the newly-established State of Israel. They proved to be exceptionally loyal friends and I always felt part of their family. They gave me love and understanding, and we developed an extraordinarily close relationship.

A NEW BEGINNING

The Halevys introduced me to their friends, Mr and Mrs Oberman, Dr Yonas and his wife, and Mr and Mrs Rosen, all of whom were to play a great part in my life for many years.

Mr and Mrs Rosen had five children. They lived in a beautiful home overlooking Brighton cricket ground and Mr Rosen liked nothing better than to sit in his special chair by the window and watch a match. After I had been staying at the Halevy's a while, the Rosens invited me to stay with them as their children were my age and there would be plenty for me to do. Reluctantly, the Halevys let me go. In the home of Mr and Mrs Rosen I was indeed to become the sixth child. Over the years, even after I married, I would go to their home as if it were my own.

Mr Rosen had a friend called Mr Jacob, who owned the local cinema. He kindly gave me a pass and I would go to the pictures at opening-time and stay there until it closed at 10.30pm. In those days, a cinema would show a 'B' film, Pathé News, and the feature film, interspersed with advertisements and trailers for the following week's programme. This would all be repeated in a continuous cycle throughout the day. That was how I learnt my English.

One evening, after about three months, we were all trying to fit into the car to go to the theatre and Mr Rosen, who was organising the seating, said to me,
"Joe, you go in the back and let Miriam sit on your lap."
"I can't do that, I'm afraid" I replied, "I have to sit in the front as my leg is in plaster and I can't bend it!"
There was a shocked silence. None of them had realised that I had an injured leg! Unceremoniously, Mr Rosen tipped us out of the car, theatre was forgotten and, indoors once again, Mr Rosen was soon on the phone to Dr Yonas who contacted orthopaedic specialists.

The following day, Mrs Oberman took me to Worthing to see a consultant. He removed the plaster and examined my leg. Within two days, I was in a private hospital, Morland Hall in Alton, Hampshire, for a week of extensive tests. By the end of the week, however, when I had expected to leave, my leg was put in traction. Morland Hall was an orthopaedic hospital that believed strongly in natural healing and, as foreign bodies can work their way to the surface, it was considered that the bullet that had been lodged in my knee for nearly two years would, if my leg were immobilised, naturally progress out towards skin level from where it could easily be removed. Incredible as it may seem, it would be four long years before I would leave Morland Hall Hospital.

I became very friendly with another survivor, Mendel, who had chest and back problems. He was to spend five years in Morland Hall. One day, he introduced me to his visitor, who immediately recognised my name.

"I've just come back from Israel and I was treated by a nursing sister who said that her maiden name was Perl."

He gave me the address of the hospital and I wrote to her straightaway. A letter came back to me by return – yes! it was my sister Sara. She wrote that she had married Victor, a baker, and that Rachel, another sister, lived nearby and worked as a secretary. I couldn't put the letter away. I read and re-read it absorbing the wonderful news. From that time, my main ambition was to see my sisters once again, and this burning desire made me increasingly restless and unable to accept the endless method of treatment.

When the doctor did his rounds one day, I grabbed his arm.

"Do something to get me out of here. Cut off my leg if you have to! I'm going to be 20 years' old soon and I've been incarcerated long enough!"

Dr McRae said he was going to perform a similar operation to the one I would need on an elderly man.

"If that operation is a success, I will operate on you", he promised.

Shortly after he came out of theatre, the doctor approached my bedside and told me that, although the operation itself had been successful, the patient had died.

"Doctor," I replied, "operate on me and I guarantee that I'll live!"

After much discussion, Dr McRae reluctantly agreed. I was taken out of traction and slowly mobilised in order to build up my muscle strength. Because I was not to put any weight on my bad leg, a four-inch-high shoe-iron was put on my good leg in order to keep my left leg off the ground and I had to use crutches. During this time, I often visited the town and got to know some of the shopkeepers. The doctor warned me that, if the operation went well, recuperation would be lengthy and I would always need crutches. The doctor was right about the former but lost a £5 bet we made together about the latter! A day or two after the operation, Dr McRae told me that my leg would never have healed as muscle had grown around the bullet, tuberculosis had set in and there had been signs of gangrene. Had I stood on it, my knee would simply have crumbled and I would have needed an amputation. Six months later, however, I left the hospital with neither crutches nor walking sticks!

During my recuperation Dr McRae, worried about my future, would sit and discuss the options that were open to me. He was concerned that I would find it difficult to cope after such a prolonged stay in hospital. I had no job, no trade, no home, no belongings, no money and, although my spoken English was fluent, I could neither write nor spell very well.

I must admit I, too, was apprehensive but I was also anxious to leave. One day when I was in town, the owner of the tailor shop beckoned me inside. While we were chatting, I told him I would soon be leaving the hospital. He was so delighted with my news that he generously offered to fit me out with new clothes even though I had no money or clothing coupons.

Dr McRae arranged a place for me at a government-funded industrial rehabilitation centre in Egham, Surrey. The centre provided accommodation and food and assessed our aptitudes. Each day, I was sent to a different section and, over the next few weeks, I was tested in many departments - light engineering, glass-making, plumbing, woodwork, metalwork, tailoring and so on. At the same time, I organised social events for the centre, and these were very successful. When my assessment was due, the Welfare Officer asked me if I would become part of the team at the centre and organise social activities on a permanent basis as I had given a new, less military, dimension to the centre and the residents' morale was raised. Many of the residents were quite severely handicapped, both physically and emotionally, mostly as a result of war injuries, and I was not ready to take on the emotional responsibility that this job, properly done, would entail. I was finding it hard enough just worrying about myself and so declined this offer.

After six weeks, I went for the results of my assessment. I was told that I had done well in all areas and was asked to choose a profession. I had met a young man who was waiting for a place on a dress-designing course. I mentioned this to the assessment team and they said it was a good choice as many Jewish people were involved in the clothing trade, and put me on a waiting list for a course in Letchworth, just north of London.

While waiting for a place to become available, the Welfare Officer found me accommodation for a week in Clapton. Eager to find out what my job opportunities would be, I went to the East End of London where I had heard there were many clothing factories. I was looking at job offer cards displayed in a window, when suddenly someone called out my name. It was Barney Oberman from Brighton!

"What are you doing here?" he cried. "How are you? When did you come out of hospital?"

I could hardly believe that in this enormous city, surrounded by strangers, here was a familiar face. We embraced warmly and I told him about my operation and the training course I was about to take.

"Come and work in my dress factory," he urged. "You can start in the cutting room, and my designer will teach you."

I was very pleased to accept the job but asked him not to tell our friends in Brighton what I was doing. I had not been in touch with them and was very anxious to stand on my own two feet before I met them again. I wanted them to feel that all the love and support they had given me had been worthwhile.

I didn't go to Letchworth and after ten days in London I received my first pay-packet – thirty shillings (£1.50)! My lodgings were £3.50 a week so I had to supplement my wages. On Saturdays, I worked in Romford markets selling men's leisurewear for a man to whom I had been introduced, and on Sundays I sold balloons in Petticoat Lane. I enrolled on a part-time dress-design course at the London Polytechnic in order to gain a City and Guild qualification. I worked by day, studied at night and, in my spare time, started a Youth Club on Thursday evenings at Leytonstone synagogue, near where I was living.

A FULL LIFE

After working for six months or so, I went to Brighton for the weekend and visited my friends there. Mrs Halevy was astonished to see me when she opened the door. She flung her arms around me and, over lunch, plied me with questions about where I was living and what I was doing.

"Why didn't you tell us where you were going after you left hospital?" she asked.

"You have all been so wonderful to me," I tried to explain, "and I wanted to come and see you on my terms, as an independent individual, to thank you for your friendship."

As I was leaving, Mrs Halevy said sincerely,

"Always remember you have a home here. Come down whenever you like."

I received the same warm greeting when I visited my other friends that weekend and from then on I went down to Brighton whenever I could afford to do so. On one visit, Mr Rosen tried to persuade me to go back and live in Brighton. I had my City and Guild qualification, but my doctor was expressing concern about my health. At that time, winter used to bring heavy black 'smogs' to London and these were affecting my lungs. He had urged me to live away from the city's pollution.

"Why do you want to live in London? Come back to Brighton. We know people who would be happy to give you a job."

So in 1952 I went to live in Brighton and worked in a dress factory. Mr and Mrs Viner had a boarding-house and I was lucky enough to have a permanent room with them. As soon as I had settled in, I became involved with youth club activities and all social events at the synagogue and before long I was part of the community. I now had many friends of my own age and my social life expanded.

I was furiously saving every penny I earned to go and meet my sisters in Israel. By 1954, I had saved enough money to travel and triumphantly booked my ticket. My boss came to me and asked,
"It is my father's ambition to go to Israel - will you take him with you?"
I had grown very close to his father who, although he was 83 years old, used to stand at my work-table for hours, reminiscing. He was a very affable gentleman, kind and understanding, and I readily agreed. We travelled by ferry and train to Marseilles, where we boarded the 'Necba', an Israeli boat which took us on to Haifa. His relations came to meet him and then I met up with my sisters. Sara, who had gone to Budapest to be a nurse, had somehow managed to avoid being rounded up and transported. When Hungary had left the Axis, Eichmann had begun his furious attempt to murder all of Hungary's Jews before the Russians arrived. Rachel had survived Auschwitz, but during her time there had been experimented on by Mengele.

What a wonderful reunion we had! I sat, a sister on each side, holding hands tightly and not wanting to let go.

After four weeks, I travelled home on the 'Jerusalem'. When I arrived at Brighton station, I was contemplating apprehensively the long walk home to my lodgings with my luggage, as I didn't even have the bus fare. As luck would have it, as I walked out of the station I met Mr Solomons, who lived opposite me.
"Hello Joe. Have you just come back from your holiday? Can I give you a lift home?"
I breathed a sigh of relief, and gratefully accepted.

Before I had gone to Israel, my friends had been trying to find me a wife. I wasn't interested - I wouldn't marry until I had seen my sisters.
"But when I get back," I confided, "the first Jewish girl who asks me to marry her - I'll marry her!"

I was on the Norwood Orphanage Committee and we were putting on a dance. I had influenza and was feeling very poorly, but the Committee chairman came to see me and said,
"Joe, you really must try to come to the dance, we need you there."

We had hired a large hall and the theme of the evening was '1984 - Big Brother is Watching You', based on George Orwell's book, which had just been televised and was hugely popular. Everyone dressed in futuristic costume, and I was on the door checking tickets when a girl came in, not wearing fancy dress as she had come straight from work. Her 21st birthday was coming up soon

131

and she had just come to hear the band, with a view to hiring them for her party. Her name was Sylvia, and although I'd never seen her before, I was intrigued to notice that everyone else seemed to know her. During the evening we danced once or twice, despite my not feeling well, but I was busy with the function and at the end of the evening when the Committee started to clear up she stayed to help us. Later, she asked if I would like a lift home as she had ordered a taxi and I didn't look at all well. In the taxi, I gave her some raffle tickets to sell as an excuse to see her again.

Nine months later we were married. We have been blessed with two wonderful children, a daughter Frances, and a son, Mark. Frances is married to Albert and they have two adorable children, Benjamin and Ella. They are my pride and joy.

My experiences have not destroyed my belief in humanity's goodness. What they have done is make me feel peripheral, always on the outside. After all these years, I still feel as if I'm in transit. I have watched the world unhinge itself and sometimes when I wake up from my nightmares I wonder - was I really that little boy who saw all that?

Thank you for listening to my story.

Josef gave a slight bow of his head and took a sip of water. I looked around at the pupils, who were sitting, without fidgeting, in absolute silence. Out of the stillness, a hand shot up.

"What happened to your Dad?"

The question came from the back of the room and I eyed the pupil thoughtfully. Michael's parents were separated and he was missing his father terribly. He would want to know how one came to terms with the loss of one's father.

Josef smiled and replied.

In the summer of 1959 I received a letter from my father. I have no idea how he had traced me. I later learned that he had returned to our home and was still living there. It was impossible, however, in those days to travel from the West to visit him. Since the war, the area had been dominated by Russia and travel was not permitted behind the 'Iron Curtain'.

Later that year, my sister Sara moved from Israel to America with her family as her eldest daughter, Rivka, had polio and they were told she would have a better chance of a full recovery there. In 1965, we received an invitation to Rivka's wedding and, as this was the first wedding of the next generation of our family, we were determined to be together. Sylvia and I saved furiously and we took our children, then aged seven and four, to Philadelphia for this joyous occasion.

After the weekend of the wedding, Sara and I talked incessantly about visiting our father. When my family and I returned home, Sara and I corresponded constantly and over the next few months it was arranged that, as travel to Bochkov was not permitted, Sara, Rachel and myself would meet in Budapest in May 1966, and my father would try to obtain a travel document and join us there.

We only had two weeks in Budapest and were waiting anxiously for news of his arrival. A week passed before he called to say that he was on his way and would arrive at 8.30 the following evening. Our father was coming! I had not seen him for 26 years, I had been 10 years old when he last saw me – would we recognise one another? My sisters and I spaced ourselves along the platform so as not to miss him amongst the crowd. Eventually the great charging monster from behind the Iron Curtain, flags flying, came smoking into the station, crashing to a halt with an impressive rush of steam. Everyone started to pile out and, as the crowds cleared, the three of us stood despondently on the empty platform gazing at each other. Had he missed the train? Been turned back? We knew he wouldn't get another chance. There were two entrances to the station and we had entered through the one without stairs because of my leg. As we began to leave, I said,
"I'm going to look at the other entrance."
"Joe," argued Sara, "with your bad leg you shouldn't climb those stairs."
"I've got to. If I don't I'll always wonder if he went that way."

When we reached the top of the stairs, I noticed a tall, slim man carrying a guitar and a suitcase. He looked so alone that I went up to him.
"Excuse me, Sir. Can I help you?"
"I don't know. I'm waiting for my son and daughters."

As he spoke he turned and I realised that I was speaking to my own father. He looked so different, so unlike the man that I had last seen in the Polish forest so long ago, but there was something about him that I immediately recognised. I was speechless as he looked blankly at me. I was a total stranger to him. He had last seen a child in the dark and now here I was, a man standing in front of him, looking him in the eyes, not up at him as a little boy. All I could say was, "Dad!"

Over the next few days we gradually got to know each other a little and tried to fill in the gaps since we had last seen one another. We exchanged our sad news about those who were no longer with us, and talked about others who had come into our lives. I gave him a photograph of my wife and children, his grandchildren, and he told me of his new wife and child. I discovered I was no longer his only son, and realised that another Perl had played in the garden where I had sat and wept for my murdered mother and sisters.

Also living near our father in Bochkov was Devorah, another sister who had survived. She had a son, a daughter and three grandchildren, and also managed to come to Budapest a couple of days later. The guitar my father carried was a gift for my son Mark. We parted after a week, Sara to America, Rachel to Israel, our father and Devorah back to Bochkov, and I returned to my life in England.

While we had been together, my Dad told me nothing of what had happened to him in the war years, but he did say that after the war he had recovered our Sefer Torah, which he had buried for safekeeping. In 1975, when my sister Devorah emigrated to Israel, he entrusted it to her to pass on to me. It had been in our family for generations and as the eldest son it was my privilege and responsibility to look after it. I was reluctant to accept it as I hoped that one day my father would be able to live in Israel, in true freedom, and in 1977 our dreams came true when he was allowed to leave Russia. That autumn, we celebrated his 86th birthday together in Israel. The Torah had been kept safely in Rachel's apartment and we brought it to him.

"While you live, father, you should use it."

"No, Josef," he replied. "I want you to take it home with you, to the synagogue where you pray."

I covered the Sefer Torah with a large blanket and carried it on my shoulder through customs at Heathrow. No-one asked me what I was carrying, no-one even seemed to notice. When I arrived home I put it away for a while as it needed considerable attention – several parchments needed replacing - and a suitably qualified scribe would be needed to restore it. Only then would we be able to use it for prayer in the synagogue. A few years later, Rabbi Benarroch took up the rabbinical post in Bournemouth, where we had been living since 1969, and we discovered that he was also a scribe.

The Sefer Torah was eventually repaired and fit to use once again. The administrators wanted us to dedicate the scroll in the synagogue at Rosh Hashanah, the Jewish New Year, as it would have been a most appropriate time for the Torah to make a new beginning, but it proved impossible for us to organise this and the ceremony was finally arranged for the Sabbath following 'Simchat Torah', when the very first portion of Genesis is read. Sarah came from America and Rachel brought her daughter from Israel for the occasion. Rachel brought a beautiful blue velvet cover for the scroll with the names of our mother and our four sisters who had perished in the Holocaust embroidered in gold. Sarah brought a silver pointer, which her children had proudly chosen, to be used when reading the Sefer Torah. I carried the Sefer Torah into the synagogue with pride and we circled the aisles for all to see. Then the first portion of the Torah was read from my scroll. It was 1983, and this event coincided with the first anniversary of my father's death, a fitting tribute to his memory.

QUESTION TIME

It was time for questions. Hands were raised around the room, and he indicated one girl, who asked,
"Have you met anyone you were in the camps with?"

Yes. One day whilst living in Brighton, I was taking .my usual lunchtime stroll when I noticed a man and a little girl of about eight years old standing on a corner as if they were waiting for someone. As I walked by them, the man spoke to me.
"Are you Joe Perl?"
"Yes. Can I help you?"
"You don't remember me, do you?"
"Should I?"

He didn't give me a direct answer, but went on to tell a long tale of how after the war he had gone to live in New Zealand, dealing in wool, and that he was on his way to Germany on business. He had stopped off in London and discovered that a Josef Perl now lived in Brighton and so he had made this journey to beg my forgiveness.
"What do I need to forgive you for?"
"We were in Bolkenhain at the same time and went on the Death March together. You carried me into Buchenwald."

"We were all so exhausted, we probably carried each other," I replied.

"You carried me, Joe. You took me into the washroom."

"Why should I forgive you for that?"

"Because, Joe, you saved my life, but I am the man who stole your bread before we left Bolkenhain!"

I remembered him well and thought back to that accursed time we had endured together. This man, whose name I do not even know, had for over twenty years longed to find me and unload the burden he carried with him.

"Of course I forgive you," I murmured reassuringly, "we're both here aren't we?"

We embraced emotionally but he had to leave for the airport straightaway, and I never saw him again.

"Do you ever think about the people who died?"

Do I think about those who died? Of course I do. I think of my mother and my sisters, of my niece and nephews, of all those children who never had a chance to live. I often wonder what the world has lost, what it will never have because those who died were on the verge of making their mark as doctors perhaps, or teachers, musicians, engineers. They all had so much to give and yet they were denied the chance. Even most of those who knew those people no longer exist. They have been wiped away as if they had never been. I, who was lucky enough to survive, have a responsibility to ensure they are never forgotten."

"Some people say that the German guards, the SS, had no choice but to obey orders."

There is always a choice between doing what is right and doing what is wrong. The real question is whether you have the strength to make that choice. Doing wrong can often be the easier option because if you don't you may be in danger, or it may make you unpopular, there are many reasons. Once your choice has been made, you can always find an excuse for what you have done, shift the blame, relinquish responsibility. Martin Gilbert, a historian, tells of German soldiers who said "No". There weren't many of them, but there were some. Most of the soldiers and all of the SS, however, fulfilled their orders with excessive zeal and often committed atrocities over and beyond their orders. A few weeks ago, I was contacted by someone who was writing a play about 'the good SS man'. I told him as far as I was concerned no such species existed.

"Do you forgive the Germans?"

Ah, forgiveness. I'm not in a position to forgive on behalf of those who are no longer here. I feel no hatred towards them because hatred is a destructive emotion. Living with hatred makes it impossible to move on so I don't hate anybody. But forgiveness is something else. It is extremely difficult to forgive a person who doesn't want to be forgiven - that, in itself, is unforgivable. I hope, however, that the generations which have followed have learned from history how to live a more tolerant life. Either way, let them ask G-d to forgive them, not me.

At this heartfelt reply the pupils sat in thoughtful silence. Josef, by saying exactly what he felt, was replying for those who could no longer speak for themselves - the owners of

140

the suitcases, the shoes the spectacles, the hair, the clothes and the toys that would never be enjoyed.

Before I go, there is one other story I would like to tell you. I was speaking at another school and, when I was leaving, a little coloured girl came up to me and said,
"Mr Perl, thank you for telling your story. No-one in this school has ever done to me what people did to you, but some are very unkind in the things they say to me and when they ignore me I know it's because I'm not like them. You have helped me realise that I can overcome all that by just being myself. We are all different from each other and our differences shouldn't really matter. Those to whom it does matter are the ones who have the real problem... and it's with themselves."

Then she hugged me and ran off. Remember that little girl - the future belongs to her as well as to you. My friends were denied their futures. When I look at you I see them as they were, as they could have been. I ask you, adopt them, take their names into your hearts, and say a prayer for those who cannot pray for themselves. Do as I do, light a candle for them and do not forget to remember them. If they are forgotten they die again. You can make sure that such a catastrophe never recurs. You are their future - you are the future!

Reluctantly I drew the session to a close. "Thank you" was said but never had those words seemed so inadequate.

DEAR MR PERL...

The whole year group assembled in the Hall and watched a play performed by some of the pupils. Each teacher in charge of the different activities gave a summing-up and comments were invited from the pupils. The usual responses were called out: "Great", "Better than normal lessons!" Isa Brysh, a retired teacher, herself a Survivor, gave a short, inspiring talk to the pupils to round off the day. Then, when I was about to begin thanking our guests, a voice called out.
"Excuse me, Sir, may I say a few words, please?"
I indicated with my hand for Josef to speak.

"I'd just like to thank you for inviting us here today. For a long time we Survivors were ignored, told our stories were too incredible to believe, that we were too emotional. It's only in the last few years that people like yourselves have asked us to tell our stories to your pupils."

While he was saying this, the other Survivors were nodding their heads. Josef was obviously reflecting their own feelings. He continued.

"We want you to know how grateful we are to be given the chance to speak, and we want to say thank you to the boys and girls for listening so politely. Thank you."

He nodded and stepped back. For a short moment there was silence and then one or two of the pupils started to applaud, and soon they were all clapping enthusiastically. It was the loud, spontaneous response of uninhibited teenagers letting us know how much the guests' contribution to 'Difference Day' had been appreciated.

After a minute or so I stopped the applause. Soon the school bell would ring and send the pupils home.
"If you would like to write to any of the guests," I said, "please let me have the letters as soon as you can as it's nearly the end of term. Kindly remain in your seats until our guests have left."

One of my colleagues escorted them out, along corridors that would soon resemble the 'Charge of the Light Brigade'. It never ceases to amaze me how quickly 900 teenagers can disappear! I walked slowly back along the now-deserted corridors to my classroom.

'Difference Day' was over, and what a day it had been, I could not remember a day like it. I felt emotionally drained, although all I had done was sit and listen to someone tell a story. Why then was I feeling so exhausted? The pupils had left about ten minutes ago and the guests had departed not long after them, eager to make their way home before the evening traffic built up. Suddenly, I realised there was a small pile of papers on my desk with a brief note on top.
"Sir, could you forward these for us please?"

The first letters had already arrived. There were to be many, many more.

"Dear Josef Perl..."

As I sat there reading the letters, I reflected on the lunchtime conversation I had had with Josef. We had skirted around the camps and details of Mr Perl's time in them, chatting instead about Bournemouth, a town with which we were both familiar. During the conversation, Josef had questioned, as have many Survivors, why it was that he had survived when so many had not.

Here, in untidy adolescent handwriting, were a variety of reasons why.

"You have made me grateful for my life"... *"Your talk has had more of an effect on me than reading books or watching videos"*... *"I felt that we actually were there"*... *"You have taught me about mankind's mistakes. I will try to stop it ever happening again."*
These children, instead of dashing off home to football, to music, to computers, had taken the time to stay in school for a few minutes and write down how they felt.

I had thought that the following day was going to be an anticlimax of the type with which we are all familiar when something one has spent so long arranging has come and gone. This was not to be the case, however, as a continual stream of pupils arrived with letters to be forwarded to the various participants in 'The Day'. Some were typed, others were hand-written on a variety of paper, from pages torn out of exercise books to scented paper probably given as a birthday gift, some were even illustrated.

144

Arranging them into containers for each of the participants so that I could read them before they were sent, I could see I had quite a task ahead of me. The pupils often wanted to discuss their letters. Some asked if the day was to be repeated next year so their younger siblings and friends could experience it, and one or two even went so far as to ask if they could take part! A quick read of some of the letters showed that they fell into well-defined categories. Some pupils thanked the speakers for a most thought-provoking day and others were more personal. As I read those to Mr Perl, I could see that Josef had made as much of an impression on the pupils as he had on me.

I reflected upon something Josef had said yesterday.
"Sometimes when Sylvia is out, or when I'm sitting watching TV, my body is in my chair but my mind is somewhere else."
Without him going into detail, one could imagine just where he was at those times. His story had made it very plain that his early life was still very much a part of him. Those of his family he had lost were like the missing pieces of a jigsaw puzzle - one could ignore the holes if one concentrated on another part of the picture but the holes were still there, one couldn't pretend they weren't. Josef and Sylvia's children and grandchildren had uncles, aunts, cousins, and grandparents that they would never know.

Each pupil had been affected by a different detail of the story. One girl wrote,
"When you were talking, my friend kept asking me if she had heard it right. Of course she had, but we didn't want to believe it..."
Another penned,

"The part of your story that moved me the most was that about the way that the soldier murdered the baby. You see, I have a new baby brother... Never have I heard such an upsetting and horrific a tale, it almost seemed unreal. Many of our group felt like crying for you and your family. You told it in a way that made us feel that we were there, watching what was happening."

Many of the letters explained how they had learnt not merely facts, but something intangible, which had been absorbed by the pupils and would be used in working out their individual philosophy of life. What Josef had achieved by telling his story was what teachers hoped for - that what they taught would help shape the individual.
"It made me realise..." (a phrase repeated again and again)
"how important one's family is..."

"...how trivial my problems are..."

"...it isn't easy to live without someone to love..."

The list went on and on and on. There were those who were convinced that 'The Day' was one of the most important in their life.
"I promise that from now on when places like Bosnia come up in the news I will have a different attitude to what is happening there..."

"You have made me realise how even what seems like a little teasing in the playground can escalate into mindless bullying with devastating results for the victim..."

"I told my parents all about you, Mr Perl, and I think that they have learnt something as well."

One feature of the letters became clear: it was not just the story that had made an impression, but the storyteller.

"I think that you are an incredible man to have the courage and strength to talk about your horrific past to a room full of strangers, not knowing whether or not it will change their outlook on life."

It obviously was changing lives.

"I believe that people like you are an asset to the world..."

"I felt a very strong sense of forgiveness in your voice, and there was a lack of anger which I found really hard to understand."

There were letters from those with a mature outlook on life,
"The most important thing that I have learnt from you is that there is a potential for evil in us all..."

"We never stop to think how our selfish behaviour can have an effect on innocent people who have done nothing wrong."

And there were those from pupils who, with a naïve approach, said just as much as their more fluent classmates,
"I feel proud of you, that you got away, but I feel guilty about what happened, I don't know why. But I will make sure that it never happens again..."

"You may not remember me. My name is Carol and I was sitting at the end of the second row." Such was the impression made that the girl was convinced he had been talking to her, and that hopefully he would remember her. "One morning I didn't have any breakfast and when I got to school I felt really hungry. I can't imagine how it must have

147

felt to be hungry for so long."   *She finished her letter by telling her friend Josef, "I am sure that telling us your story must take a lot out of you but thank you for sharing it with us. I will never forget you."*

"I have thought a lot about your story and it has changed my way of thinking for ever... I have learned that anything is possible in life... I feel a lot stronger, understanding how important it is to help and respect those around you.   Life has been given a new meaning and I know how precious it is."

I read on.
"Thank you so much... Your talk showed the people behind the statistics and I learnt far more than I could have in class."

"No amount of videos or textbooks could have brought home to us how the mass destruction of millions of Jews affected each individual survivor like your talk did."

"It probably sounds weird, but I was sitting there listening to you and I couldn't help but think how you looked like my Grandad and that you are the same age, and it's sickening to think that if his religion was Judaism and he had lived in Europe he would have gone through and suffered as you did but he may not have survived.   Consequently the generations after my Grandad would not be here – neither would I!"

"I thought you were very brave and I hope that my generation and all future generations will never experience what you went through."

148

"Your final message of "do not be nasty to each other" really means something to me as I have been bullied since I started going to school about the colour of my hair – ginger."

"I think everybody should learn about the Holocaust because it teaches everyone that to prevent it happening again, we need to create peace in the world which will begin with people loving their family and friends."

"Twenty-six years separated from anyone in my family would be 'mindboggling' – I can't even live without them for a month."

"I hope that through your spoken and written accounts of the Holocaust we will learn the evils that genocide and racial hatred can cause."

"After the Holocaust I am shocked that violence still occurs in the world. Why haven't people learnt from past mistakes?"

"I wondered how I would have coped and what I would have done if I was alive at that time, and found that I honestly did not know, which was a very sobering thought and it scared me."

Josef Perl, by telling his story, had educated the pupils in a way that they would carry with them for the rest of their lives. In him, they saw the strength of a Survivor, the invincibility of his courage, his unshakeable belief in man's inherent goodness, his lack of hatred and bitterness and his unwavering belief in his own personal G-d. After ten years of unspeakable suffering, torture, injury and finally

149

hospitalisation, he had emerged at the age of twenty still independent and in control of his future. He built a family of his own and also a wider family of students around the country, which continues to grow as he talks of faces in the smoke.